UNIVERSITY OF NORTH CAROLINA AT CHAPEL HILL

DEPARTMENT OF ROMANCE LANGUAGES

NORTH CAROLINA STUDIES
IN THE ROMANCE LANGUAGES AND LITERATURES

ESSAYS; *TEXTS, TEXTUAL STUDIES AND TRANSLATIONS*; SYMPOSIA

Founder: URBAN TIGNER HOLMES

Distributed by:

UNIVERSITY OF NORTH CAROLINA PRESS
CHAPEL HILL
North Carolina 27514
U.S.A.

NORTH CAROLINA STUDIES IN THE
ROMANCE LANGUAGES AND LITERATURES
Essays
Number 8

THE NOVELS OF MME RICCOBONI

THE NOVELS OF MME RICCOBONI

BY
JOAN HINDE STEWART

CHAPEL HILL

NORTH CAROLINA STUDIES IN THE ROMANCE
LANGUAGES AND LITERATURES
U.N.C. DEPARTMENT OF ROMANCE LANGUAGES
1976

Library of Congress Cataloging in Publication Data

Stewart, Joan Hinde.
    The novels of Mme Riccoboni.

    (North Carolina studies in the Romance languages and literatures: Essays; no. 8)
    Originally presented as the author's thesis, Yale.
    Bibliography: p. 154.
    1. Riccoboni, Marie Jeanne de Heurles Laboras de Mézières, 1713-1792—Criticism and interpretation.
I. Title. II. Series.

PQ2027.R3Z86   1974   843'.5   75-4822
ISBN: 978-0-80789-165-0

DEPÓSITO LEGAL: V. 4.196 - 1975

ARTES GRÁFICAS SOLER, S. A. - JÁVEA, 28 - VALENCIA (8) - 1976

To
my mother
and to
the memory of
my father

FOREWORD

This study was originally prepared as a doctoral dissertation for Yale University. My thanks to Georges May, who suggested the topic and gave constant and sympathetic guidance and encouragement in its preparation, to Charles Porter and to Sandy Petrey for their careful reading of the manuscript, to James Nicholls for making available to me the manuscript of his edition of Mme Riccoboni's letters; to the Ford Foundation, which provided a summer grant in 1971 so that I could undertake additional research to the Faculty Research and Professional Development Fund of North Carolina State University; and to Philip Stewart for his patient advice and criticism and his unfailing support.

TEXTUAL NOTE

References to the works of Mme Riccoboni are to the 1781 edition of her collected works, published by Humblot (Paris) in eight volumes. (A ninth volume, containing four short stories, was added in 1783.) This edition is actually a collection of earlier separate editions which Humblot gathered together as a whole. In addition to the 1781 title page at the head of each volume, each individual work has its own title page bearing the earlier date of publication. The following list gives the full titles of the works as they appear in this collection, along with the publication date borne by each individual title page and, in parentheses, the original date of publication.

Volume	Title	
I	*Lettres de Mylady Juliette Catesby à Mylady Henriette Campley, son amie.* 1769	(1759)
	Lettres de Mistriss Fanni Butlerd à Milord Charles Alfred, Comte d'Erford. 1772	(1757)
II	*Histoire de Monsieur le Marquis de Cressy.* 1772	(1758)
	Histoire d'Ernestine. 1772	(1765)
	Recueil de pièces détachées (L'Abeille, Suite de Marianne, et al.). 1772	
III	*Amélie.* 1781	(1762)

IV	*Histoire de Miss Jenny, écrite et envoyée par elle à Mylady, Comtesse de Roscomonde, Ambassadrice d'Angleterre à la Cour de Dannemarck.* 1775	(1764)
V	*Lettres d'Élisabeth-Sophie de Vallière à Louise-Hortence de Canteleu, son amie.* 1775	(1771)
VI	*Lettres d'Adélaïde de Dammartin, Comtesse de Sancerre, à Monsieur le Comte de Nancé, son ami.* 1771	(1766)
	Lettres de Mylord Rivers à Sir Charles Cardigan, entremêlées d'une partie de ses correspondances à Londres pendant son séjour en France. 1777	(1776)
VII & VIII	*Le Nouveau Théâtre anglais.* 1769	(1768-69)
IX	*Histoire de Christine, Reine de Suabe, et celle d'Aloïse de Livarot; Histoire d'Enguerrand, et celle des Amours de Gertrude.* 1783	(1779-80)

References to the English correspondence of Mme Riccoboni are based on James C. Nicholls, *Mme Riccoboni's Letters to David Hume, David Garrick and Sir Robert Liston: 1764-1783* (forthcoming), and are designated by the abbreviation "N" with the number of the letter in that edition, e. g. (N. 53); other letters, identified only by date, are based on an unpublished doctoral dissertation by the same author, "A Critical Edition of the Correspondence of Mme Riccoboni" (University of Wisconsin, 1962).

In quoting Mme Riccoboni's works and correspondence, I have used twentieth-century spelling and punctuation. All italics are in the original. Three dots which appear unspaced in the text do not represent my ellipses, but stylistic *points de suspension* in the original.

References to the letter-novels will be given by Roman numeral, indicating the number of the letter quoted.

TABLE OF CONTENTS

	Page
TEXTUAL NOTE	11

CHAPTER
- I. ACTRESS TURNED AUTHOR 15
- II. NARRATION THROUGH LETTERS: TECHNICAL CONSIDERATIONS 36
- III. THE LETTER'S MANY MEANINGS: *FANNI BUTLERD*. 57
- IV. VARIATIONS ON A FORMULA 79
- V. THE EGOCENTRIC MALE 101
- VI. WOMANHOOD: SENSE AND SENSIBILITY 120

A SELECTED BIBLIOGRAPHY 154

CHAPTER I

ACTRESS TURNED AUTHOR

> Faites-leur des ouvrages bien doux, bien tendres,
> remplis d'esprit, de goût et de sensibilité.
> —Diderot to Mme Riccoboni
> November 27, 1758

Mme Riccoboni was not Italian, as her name would suggest, but a Frenchwoman — the widow of an Italian actor — who lived her entire life in Paris. She began her own career as an actress at the Comédie Italienne, but eventually abandoned the stage to write novels and became, along with Mme de Graffigny and Mlle de Lussan, one of the most successful female authors of the century. Her first three novels — *Lettres de Mistriss Fanni Butlerd* (1757), *Histoire du Marquis de Cressy* (1758) and *Lettres de Mylady Juliette Catesby* (1759) — rapidly attained the status of best-sellers and catapulted her into a position of prominence both in France and abroad; by the end of the century, her works had gone through numerous French editions and been translated into all the major languages of Europe.[1] Several American editions

---

[1] At least twenty editions of *Lettres de Juliette Catesby* alone had appeared by 1800, and the novel had been translated into English, Italian, Danish, Swedish and Russian. See Angus Martin, "Romans et romanciers à succès," *Revue des Sciences Humaines*, 139 (1970), 388, Emily Crosby, *Une Romancière oubliée* (Paris, 1924), pp. 175-83, and Paul Van Tieghem, "Le Roman sentimental en Europe de Richardson à Rousseau (1740-1761)," *Revue de Littérature comparée*, 20 (1940), 145. Emily Crosby's work, uneven in quality and largely biographical in orientation, is nonetheless the only full-length study of Mme Riccoboni to date, and has provided material for my own work.

even appeared around the turn of the century in as surprising a place as New Bern, North Carolina.[2]

So highly regarded were her novels that the dilettantish satirist Charles Palissot, among others, found it difficult to accept her authorship of them. He put Mme Riccoboni in his *Dunciade* of 1764, designating her as a member of the entourage of Stupidity:

> Elle y viendra cette Rubiconi,
> Qui n'a point fait le Marquis de Cressy,
> Qui n'a point fait Les Lettres de Fanny,
> Qui n'a point fait Juliette Catesby.[3]

Palissot's ridicule notwithstanding, she had the wholehearted admiration of some of her most important literary contemporaries. Diderot wrote of her in 1769, "cette femme écrit comme un ange; c'est un naturel, une pureté, une sensibilité, une élégance qu'on ne saurait trop admirer."[4] Adam Smith placed her in a class with Voltaire, Racine and Marivaux as one of the "poets and romance writers who best paint the refinements of love and friendship, and of all other private and domestic affections."[5] Such unlikely people as Choderlos de Laclos and Restif de la Bretonne were likewise devoted admirers of Mme Riccoboni.

A more recent work dealing with another aspect of Mme Riccoboni is James C. Nicholls, *Mme Riccoboni's Letters to David Hume, David Garrick and Sir Robert Liston: 1764-1783* (forthcoming). The present study is greatly indebted to Mr. Nicholls for making the letters of Mme Riccoboni accessible and for providing invaluable biographical information and commentary, both in the published correspondence and in his unpublished doctoral dissertation (University of Wisconsin, 1962) on the same subject.

[2] See James C. Nicholls, "Mme Riccoboni in North Carolina," *Revue de Littérature comparée*, 41 (1967), 285-88.

[3] Charles Palissot de Montenoy, *La Dunciade ou la Guerre des sots* (Chelsea, 1764), p. 88. A footnote to the text reads, "Ce sont les titres de trois petits romans dont le public s'obstine à ne pas reconnaître l'auteur." Palissot later recanted but his initial refusal to credit Mme Riccoboni with the works was symptomatic of a problem which would plague her as a female writer: after her death, her friend Mlle Biancolelli wrote in a letter to La Harpe, "Dès qu'elle fut connue, on lui disputa ses ouvrages; c'est la règle surtout à l'égard des femmes" (J.-F. de La Harpe, *Œuvres* [Paris, 1820-21], XV, 524).

[4] Denis Diderot, *Œuvres complètes*, ed. J. Assézat (Paris: Garnier, 1875-77), VIII, 465.

[5] *Theory of Moral Sentiments*, 6th ed. (London: Strahan and Cadell, 1790), I, 350.

Laclos wrote the lyrics to a comic-opera based on the Riccoboni novel *Histoire d'Ernestine* (performed only once, in July 1777 at the Comédie Italienne, it was a complete failure); later he paid her the tribute of expending much effort and large quantities of ink in order to improve her opinion of *Les Liaisons dangereuses*.[6] Restif, for his part, lavished praise on her work and, in an interesting commentary on women authors, declared that she alone among them was not to be disdained:

> Que je plains la femme auteur ou savante! Jeunes personnes, elle est réellement à plaindre. Elle a perdu le charme de son sexe; c'est un homme parmi les femmes, et ce n'est pas une femme parmi les hommes ... A moins que, prudente comme la sage Riccoboni, elle ne soit restée dans un genre convenable à son sexe, dans ce genre aimable, moral, quoique léger, où le style de femme se fait sentir, malgré les audacieux détracteurs qui ont voulu lui enlever sa gloire. Je défie à un homme, quelqu'il soit, de faire les *Lettres de Catesby*, et même les *Lettres de Fanny Buttler*. Il les imitera, mais de loin; jamais il ne fera de même, fût-il Voltaire, et y mît-il toute sa capacité. Mais Riccoboni est la seule qui ait cette manière de sexe, châtiée, sans pédanterie et parfaitement agréable.[7]

During the early part of his career, Restif tried to imitate Mme Riccoboni's manner of writing, pronouncing himself discouraged by the excellence of her work.[8]

The Italian poet and playwright, Goldoni, who was her neighbor in Paris in 1762, translated her work into Italian and noted in his memoirs that she had delighted all Paris with novels "dont la pureté du style, la délicatesse des images, la vérité des passions, et l'art d'intéresser et d'amuser en même temps, la mettaient au pair avec tout ce qu'il y a d'estimable dans la Littérature Française."[9] Later in the century, Goethe's Charlotte in

---

[6] See below, pp. 23-24.

[7] *Les Françaises*, in *L'Œuvre*, ed. Henri Bachelin (Paris: Editions du Trianon, 1930-32), II, 346.

[8] See Charles A. Porter, *Restif's Novels* (New Haven: Yale University Press, 1967), pp. 28, 43.

[9] Carlo Goldoni, *Mémoires pour servir à l'histoire de sa vie et à celle de son théâtre* (Paris: Duchesne, 1787), III, 12.

Werther mentions *Histoire de Miss Jenny* as one of the novels in which she most delighted as a young girl.[10] Mme de Genlis found the heroine of *Lettres de Fanni Butlerd* lacking in decency and devoid of charm, and labeled the suicide in *Histoire du Marquis de Cressy* "revolting," but in spite of these reservations, she had enormous admiration for the author and believed that her star outshone even Prévost's:

> Avant que madame Riccoboni eût écrit, les romans de l'abbé Prévost jouissoient d'une grande réputation; mais ceux de madame Riccoboni en ont rendu la lecture impossible, et nul ouvrage de ce genre ne fera tomber dans l'oubli les *Lettres de Milady Catesby, Ernestine, Jenny, Amélie,* etc.[11]

Sainte-Beuve tells us that Marie-Antoinette's predilection for Mme Riccoboni led her to disguise her novels as books of hours, the better to read them during services.[12]

Eighteenth-century literary reviews by and large agreed with these evaluations. In 1765 the *Correspondance littéraire* remarked that, "un ton distingué, un style élégant, léger et rapide, la mettront toujours au-dessus de toutes les femmes qui ont jugé à propos de se faire imprimer en ces derniers temps."[13] Reviewing *Histoire du Marquis de Cressy, L'Année littéraire* commented, "Tout décèle un auteur à qui les mœurs du monde et les routes du cœur sont également connues."[14] In his *Essai de Littérature à l'usage des dames,* published in 1794, Dampmartin declared,

> Il appartenait à Me Riccoboni de marcher avec éclat dans une route aussi battue. Ses ouvrages, pleins d'esprit, respirent à chaque page une sensibilité que nul homme

---

[10] "Weiss Gott, wie wohl mir's war, wenn ich mich Sonntags in so ein Eckchen setzen und mit ganzen Herzen an dem Glück und Unstern einer Miss Jenny teilnehmen konnte" (*Goethes Werke* [Hamburg, 1965], VI, 23).

[11] *De l'Influence des femmes sur la littérature française* (Paris, 1811), p. 278.

[12] *Nouveaux Lundis* (Paris: Michel Lévy, 1865-84), VIII (1867), 346.

[13] *Correspondance littéraire, philosophique et critique,* ed. Maurice Tourneux (Paris: Garnier, 1877-82), VI (May 1765), 275-76.

[14] *L'Année littéraire,* 1758, IV, 128.

ne parviendrait à exprimer avec autant de délicatesse.
Les *Lettres de Juliette Catesby* resteront toujours comme
un chef-d'œuvre de naturel et de grâce. [15]

It was, in fact, *Lettres de Juliette Catesby* which received the
most enthusiastic notices and was to attain the greatest success.
The Abbé de Laporte said that Catesby's letters "paraissent
dictées par le sentiment; et l'esprit en est puisé dans la nature
même," [16] while the *Correspondance littéraire* called the novel a
"petit chef-d'œuvre de perfection" and added: "Un auteur qui
n'aurait jamais fait d'autre preuve de talent ne pourrait pas être
effacé de la liste des écrivains distingués d'une nation." [17] Fréron
in *L'Année littéraire* loudly applauded the work, ending his review
with the following remark: "Depuis plus de six ans, je n'ai rien
lu dans ce genre frivole d'aussi bien écrit et d'aussi intéressant.
Ah, M. Rousseau de Genève, que direz-vous, lorsque vous apprendrez
que l'auteur de ce Roman est une femme?" [18] Still
further indications of Mme Riccoboni's prestige are to be found
in the works which attempted to ride the wave of her popularity [19]:
for example, the title page of a rather banal novel of
1760, *Mémoires de Milédi B...*, by Mlle de la Guesnerie, announces
its author as "Mme R..." and an "Avis du libraire"
reads, "L'accueil que le Public a fait aux Lettres de *Mistriss
Fanni*, et à celles de *Miladi Juliette*, m'ont engagé à lui présenter
les *Mémoires de Milédi B...* Je serai satisfait s'il les reçoit avec
autant d'empressement." [20]

* * *

Little remembered today, Mme Riccoboni was one of the most
admired and widely read authors of her day; yet for all her

---

[15] Anne-Henri Cabet, vicomte de Dampmartin, *Essai de littérature à
l'usage des dames* (Amsterdam: G. Heintzen, 1794), II, 48.
[16] *Histoire littéraire des femmes françaises, ou Lettres historiques et
critiques* (Paris: Lacombe, 1769), V, 33.
[17] IX (February 1772), 451.
[18] 1758, VIII, 302.
[19] Cf. Crosby, p. 154.
[20] The attribution of this novel is doubtful, but both Henri Coulet
(*Le Roman jusqu'à la Révolution* [Paris: Armand Colin, 1967], II, 379)
and Laurent Versini (*Laclos et la tradition* [Paris: Klincksieck, 1968], p. 111)
attribute the work to Mlle de la Guesnerie.

popularity as a novelist, her contemporaries knew little about her private existence and much of what they thought to be true of her was not. She herself preferred for the most part to keep silent about her background: when Philip Thicknesse, an Englishman whose wife was preparing a book about the lives of French women of letters, wrote to Mme Riccoboni in 1780 asking for a portrait and a résumé of her life, she refused. "Des particularités sur ma vie," she responded, "formeraient un article bien insipide et bien peu étendu ... Je suis fâchée, Monsieur, de n'avoir point une histoire intéressante à vous raconter. La vie d'une femme sensée offre rarement des faits dignes d'attention, la mienne n'a pas été heureuse." The details of her life came to light in 1872 with the publication of an article on her in Auguste Jal's *Dictionnaire critique*.

Marie-Jeanne de Heurles de Laboras was born in Paris on October 25, 1713 under rather unpropitious circumstances. The marriage of her bourgeois parents was illegal: eight months after her birth their union was declared null and her father was excommunicated for bigamy. Until the age of fourteen, she was raised in a convent; she would later energetically attack the education she received there as completely inappropriate: "On ne m'enseigna rien, on fit de moi une bonne petite dévote, propre seulement à prier Dieu, puisque Satan la forçait de renoncer à ses pompes" (N. 78). With her mother, who was still young and rather jealous of her attractive daughter, her relationship was none too good; on July 7, 1734, she escaped her unhappy home life by a marriage to her neighbor, Antoine-François Riccoboni. "J'écoutai le premier homme qui me fit espérer une société plus douce," she wrote to the English actor David Garrick, "je me mariai pour quitter ma mère" (N. 78). Her marriage proved a dismal failure; the tempestuous Antoine-François inflicted on his wife many senseless debts which he accumulated. In another letter to Garrick, she said of him: "il se conduit à soixante ans comme un homme de vingt et c'est moi qui paye ses sottises" (N. 53). His death notice in Bachaumont's *Mémoires secrets* says unabashedly that "il vivait dans la débauche et la crapule; il était même accusé de pédérastie." [21] Bachaumont's opinion is not

---

[21] *Mémoires secrets* (London: Adamson, 1780), VI (May 26, 1772), 142.

necessarily reliable, but in fact few contemporary documents reflect to Riccoboni's credit. His wife sought a more congenial companion and in 1755 took up residence with her friend and sister-actress, Marie-Thérèse Biancolelli; the two lived together harmoniously on the rue Poissonnière until the author's death in 1792.

By her marriage to Riccoboni, Marie-Jeanne did, nonetheless, gain entrance into one of the most illustrious theatrical families of the day: her husband was the son of the actress Flaminia and of the celebrated Luigi Riccoboni (better known by the stage name of Lélio), who had brought the Comédie Italienne back to Paris in 1716 at the invitation of the Regent. Antoine-François was himself a playwright and an actor in his father's troupe. Six weeks after their wedding, Marie-Jeanne (de Mézières, as she called herself then) made her stage début as Lucile, the female lead in Louis de Boissy's *La Surprise de la haine*. The performance was well received and she was accepted as a member of the company a few months later; by all reports, nonetheless, she seems to have been a mediocre actress. She herself wrote to Garrick that, "actrice intelligente et froide, je n'ai pas brillé dans l'art où vous excellez" (N. 78). Diderot cites her example in *Paradoxe sur le comédien* to illustrate his thesis that persons of real sensitivity do not make great actors; an actor, he insists, must persuade the public of his genuineness not by being genuine but by means of his art:

> Cette femme, une des plus sensibles que la nature ait formées, a été une des plus mauvaises actrices qui ait jamais paru sur la scène. Personne ne parle mieux de l'art, personne ne joue plus mal.... C'est parce qu'elle est constamment restée elle que le public l'a constamment dédaignée. [22]

Another of her contemporaries, Voisenon, likewise paid her a strangely mixed compliment when he wrote: "on devrait lui donner une pension, pour la récompenser d'avoir quitté le théâtre, où elle jouait fort mal, et de s'appliquer à faire de très jolis

---

[22] *Œuvres complètes*, VIII, 410-11.

romans."[23] She remained an actress, in spite of her limited success, for a period of twenty-seven years: it was only in 1761 that the proceeds from her first three novels permitted her to retire.

After Mme Riccoboni began to publish in 1757, her reputation as an author brought her into contact with many noteworthy personalities of the day, and her correspondence bears testimony to the warmth and duration of the friendships she formed. She was for many years a frequent visitor at the salon of Baron d'Holbach, where she met prominent Frenchmen and visitors from abroad. Here, presumably, she became acquainted with Denis Diderot, to whom she submitted her manuscripts for commentary and who wrote a detailed critique of one of them,[24] and David Hume, who helped to arrange for the English translation of *Histoire de Miss Jenny*. Of all the acquaintances which she made in the mid 60's, probably the most important were those of David Garrick and Sir Robert Liston. Most of her extant correspondence is addressed to these two men and this correspondence contains some of her finest pages, revealing her as a devoted friend and a passionate, spontaneous, and occasionally caustic and irreverent woman.

David Garrick, who for many years managed the Drury Lane theatre and who brought Shakespeare back to life in eighteenth-century England, met Mme Riccoboni when he and his wife visited Paris in 1763-64. She developed a lasting affection for Garrick and they corresponded for some fifteen years, even though they never again saw one another.[25] Garrick performed many services for her during this time, overseeing the English translations of her novels and supplying her with the latest English works to appear. In turn, she translated into French his play *The*

---

[23] L'Abbé de Voisenon, *Œuvres complètes* (Paris: Moutard, 1781), IV, 148.

[24] *Lettres de Juliette Catesby*. See *Correspondance*, ed. Georges Roth and Jean Varloot (Paris: Editions de Minuit, 1956-68), II, 101-02 (November 27, 1758).

[25] For the history of Mme Riccoboni's relationship with Garrick and Liston, and for biographical information concerning all three, see Nicholls' introduction to *Mme Riccoboni's Letters to David Hume, David Garrick and Sir Robert Liston: 1764-1783*.

Clandestine Marriage and dedicated to him her novel *Lettres de Madame de Sancerre*.

Her relationship with Robert Liston, a young Scot nearly thirty years her junior, was considerably more complex; while her interest in him was partly maternal, and became more so as the years went on, it seems undeniable that she was also in love with him.[26] Her correspondence provides many indications of this: in 1771, for example, she wrote to him, "Quand vous passâtes je me croyais paisible, l'amour était assoupi dans mon cœur. Vous êtes revenu. Votre présence a produit sur moi l'effet de l'air sur un feu couvert, la cendre s'est écartée et la flamme a paru avec sa première activité" (N. 63). And the following year, when she was fifty-eight years old:

> Si je m'examine sérieusement, je serai forcée de m'avouer qu'il m'est impossible de vous regarder ou de vous traiter comme un autre. Chaque année qui s'écoule ajoute au ridicule d'un attachement de cette espèce; je me moquerais fort d'une femme de mon âge qui me montrerait la même faiblesse, pourquoi donc ne me moquerais-je pas de moi, qui n'ai pu lire sans émotion deux lignes de votre main où vous exprimez un sentiment un peu plus tendre qu'à l'ordinaire? (N. 90).

Liston, who eventually became a diplomat, visited Mme Riccoboni periodically in Paris, and they kept up a regular correspondence. His letters to her have never been found, but hers to him, covering the period from 1766 to 1783, not only detail the profound attachment she felt, but also contain amusing and illuminating anecdotes about contemporary life in Paris as well as literary news and judgments. This correspondence is invaluable for the insights it provides into her philosophy, her tastes, and her ideas about writing; thematically and stylistically, moreover, the letters to Liston much resemble those of Mme Riccoboni's amorous heroines.

Towards the end of her life, Mme Riccoboni engaged in an animated exchange of letters with Choderlos de Laclos; she initiated the contact shortly after the appearance of *Les Liaisons*

---

[26] See Nicholls' introduction.

dangereuses, in order to express her disapproval of the work. She objected to the novel on patriotic as well as feministic grounds, maintaining that the character of Mme de Merteuil was a disgrace to the French nation, to the female sex and to human nature itself: "J'invite Monsieur de Laclos à ne jamais orner le vice des agréments qu'il a prêtés à Madame de Merteuil" (April 1782). One can readily appreciate her objections to the character of the Marquise when one considers the artless nature of Mme Riccoboni's own heroines, and her thesis that men are guilty of the vicious exploitation of innocent women. In a subsequent letter Mme Riccoboni's anti-male sentiments become manifest when she sternly advises Laclos that he should not risk alienating women by so insulting a portrait: "Vous ne savez pas, Monsieur, combien vous regretterez un jour leur amitié. Elle est si douce, elle devient si agréable à votre sexe, quand ses passions amorties lui permettent de ne plus les regarder comme l'objet de son amusement" (April 19, 1782). Laclos responded with a lengthy justification of his work. Several additional letters were exchanged, and the discussion might have continued indefinitely, had not Mme Riccoboni formally ended it:

> Permettez-moi donc de terminer une dispute dont nos derniers neveux ne verraient pas la fin, si elle continuait. Le brillant succès de votre livre doit vous faire oublier ma légère censure. Parmi tant de suffrages à quoi vous servirait celui d'une cénobite ignorée? Il n'ajouterait point à votre gloire. (April-May 1782)

Her last literary effort occurred a few years after the close of the Laclos correspondence: at the age of seventy-two, she composed a long short story, *Histoire de deux jeunes amies,* which appeared in the *Mercure de France* in 1786. She died in December 1792 and was buried by her loving friend Thérèse Biancolelli in the church of Saint-Eustache, site of her baptism and marriage.

* * *

It was in the epistolary novel of sentiment that Mme Riccoboni principally distinguished herself. She tried her hand at a variety of literary forms — including plays on which she collaborated with her husband, translations, journal articles, and short stories — but the main body of her work is composed of just eight novels (six of them written in letter form), published over a period of twenty years. Her career as a writer, nonetheless, actually began well before the 1757 appearance of her first novel: as early as 1751, yielding to the vogue of pastiches, she composed a *Suite* to Marivaux's incomplete *Vie de Marianne*.[27] The success of this first venture into fiction was perhaps instrumental in determining her to write novels of her own. It seems that Saint-Foix having maintained in the presence of Mme Riccoboni that Marivaux's style was inimitable, the actress rose to the challenge and produced a continuation of *La Vie de Marianne;* it consists chiefly of a meeting between the irresistible heroine and her erstwhile suitor, Valville, followed by an interview between a triumphant and disdainful Marianne and her rival, Mlle de Varthon. This was read in the presence of Saint-Foix, who was completely taken in; along with just about everyone else he believed it to be the work of Marivaux. The first half of the *Suite* was published some ten years later, with Marivaux's blessings, in *Le Monde comme il est*. Marivaux received so many compliments on the work that he was finally forced to betray the secret he had agreed to keep regarding its authorship. Although Mme Riccoboni later termed the *Suite* "une plaisanterie de société, une folie de ma jeunesse" (to Denis Humblot, 1765), Grimm called it an "imitation parfaite de la manière de Marivaux,"[28] while d'Alembert said, "On ne saurait pousser plus loin la vérité de l'imitation."[29]

Contemporary plaudits notwithstanding, it is unfortunate that Mme Riccoboni is perhaps best known today as the author of the *Suite,* for this piece of writing does not equal her own best novels and is at the same time inferior to its model. Superficially, nonetheless, the *Suite* does resemble the other divisions of *La Vie de Marianne,* and Mme Riccoboni undeniably succeeds, as

---

[27] For the history of its composition and publication, as well as a description of the *Suite* — not to be confused with an inferior production called a *Fin,* which appeared in 1742 — see Jean Fleury, *Marivaux et le marivaudage* (Paris: Plon, 1881), pp. 192-202.

[28] *Correspondance littéraire,* VI (May 1765), 275.

[29] *Histoire des membres de l'Académie française* (Paris: Moutard, 1787), VI: "Eloge de Marivaux," pp. 83-84.

Grimm explains, in capturing something of the procedure of the original author, "qui consiste à se donner un mouvement prodigieux sans avancer d'un pas" [30]: like Marivaux's Marianne, Mme Riccoboni's chats, analyses and exclaims at length, but in the end the plot has advanced little. Mme Riccoboni must also be credited, as Jean Fleury says, with creating action which is primarily interior and is resolved in the hearts of the protagonists, thus remaining faithful to Marivaux's technique. [31] But the character of Marianne changes considerably in Mme Riccoboni's hands: more overtly and self-consciously coquettish, she loses the subtlety with which Marivaux had gifted her, and there is less refinement of language and situation. While the original Marianne, for example, is aware of her attractiveness and takes pleasure in observing the effects of her charms, one can hardly imagine her unabashedly declaring, as her re-creation does, "j'ai toujours regardé avec plaisir ceux qui me distinguaient, me trouvaient belle, m'admiraient. Pourtant, que faisaient-ils, je vous prie? ils me rendaient justice: voilà tout." [32] The tone is too blunt, the nuances are lacking: this is no longer the heroine of *La Vie de Marianne*.

Just as certain of the remarks concerning men which she attributes to Marianne ("les hommes sont bien ridicules, bien inconséquents; nous ne les aimons que faute de les examiner") [33] seem more characteristic of the Riccoboni heroines than of Marianne, so too the stylistic devices most incompatible with Marivaux serve sometimes to indicate the direction Mme Riccoboni's own style would take. The use of the suspended utterance, for example, which Deloffre finds alien to the manner of Marivaux, will be a constant of *Lettres de Fanni Butlerd* and *Lettres de Juliette Catesby*. [34] Her description of a confused

---

[30] *Correspondance littéraire*, VI (May 1765), 275.

[31] *Marivaux et le marivaudage*, p. 199.

[32] Marivaux, *La Vie de Marianne*, ed. F. Deloffre (Paris: Garnier, 1963), p. 610. Mme Riccoboni's *Suite* is reproduced at the end of this volume; in his footnotes, Deloffre points out several instances where Mme Riccoboni fails to imitate Marivaux effectively, presenting instead a Marianne who is in some senses "bien déchue" (p. 605).

[33] *La Vie de Marianne*, p. 616.

[34] See chapter two of the present study.

and distraught Valville, beguiled by Marianne's charms — "Il se lève, renverse sa chaise, marche à grands pas, s'agite, ouvre une fenêtre, la renferme, revient, me regarde, retourne, se promène, respire avec peine, joint ses mains, les lève, les baisse, ne sait ce qu'il fait" [35] — has little in common with Marivaux's style, [36] but is precisely the method used by Juliette Catesby to ridicule one of her suitors: "Il va, vient, retourne, s'agite, arrache des mains de Betty tout ce qu'elle veut me présenter, dérange mes livres, les fait tomber, me demande du thé, en prépare, s'en va sans en prendre" (X). This procedure, by which a long string of verbs is used to attain a staccato effect and translate incoherence and bewilderment, has a theatrical quality typical of Mme Riccoboni's writing.

In her effort to imitate Marivaux, she demonstrates her sensitivity to style, and one of the greatest achievements of her own work is, in fact, stylistic; the journals of the period speak constantly of the liveliness of her narratives, the purity of her prose, the delicacy of her descriptions, the precision of her expressions. In its 1764 review of *Histoire de Miss Jenny*, the *Correspondance littéraire* attempted a brief résumé of the merits of Mme Riccoboni's works and particularly emphasized her style: "l'art de narrer avec beaucoup de concision et de rapidité, celui de semer dans son récit des réflexions fines et justes, beaucoup de finesse et de grâce dans le style, et un ton très distingué: voilà les principales qualités de la plume de Mme Riccoboni." [37] According to the Abbé de Laporte, "elle parle surtout le langage du cœur d'une manière si naturelle, qu'on entre, malgré soi, dans son sujet, qu'on partage la joie et la douleur des personnages qu'elle met sur la scène." [38] She is more suggestive than descriptive and the absence of external detail which characterizes her manner distinguishes her from Marivaux. More restrained, more classic than that of numerous novelists of the period, her style has in many cases aged less than theirs. It is devoid of heaviness, excessive

---

[35] *La Vie de Marianne*, pp. 604-05.
[36] "Les personnages de Marivaux ne se livrent pas à des gesticulations incohérentes" (Deloffre, p. 605).
[37] VI (June 1764), 20-21.
[38] *Histoire littéraire des femmes françaises*, V, 78.

preciosity and declamation; there are none of the clichés or grandiloquent metaphors which tend to make another feminine novel of the time, *Lettres d'une Péruvienne,* tiresome reading in our day. Mme Riccoboni's best stylistic achievement was perhaps *Lettres de Fanni Butlerd,* where form, content and tone are all extremely well suited to each other; but the directness, vibrancy and theatricality of Fanni's style (which will be discussed in chapter three) all characterize the later novels as well. Mme Riccoboni's writing appears spontaneous, never studied; if at times her expression is a trifle precious, at others it is altogether eloquent, and at still others downright drole.

In contrast to the hastily written *Suite,* her own novels were constantly reworked and polished. Passages of her correspondence indicate the significance which she attached to perfecting a work before releasing it; apropos of *Histoire de Miss Jenny,* which her editor, Humblot, urged her in 1762 to complete as rapidly as possible, assuring her he would immediately publish it, she replied,

> Vous imprimerez, d'accord; mais qui lira, je vous prie? Ne doit-on rien au public? Serait-il bien d'abuser de ses premières complaisances? Faut-il ajouter à ces défauts qui échappent toujours, une négligence volontaire? Non: il est mal de tenir un ouvrage pour fini, quand on croit pouvoir mieux faire en y travaillant encore. (Early 1762)

Mlle Biancolleli corroborates this account of her friend's work habits: "Très difficile pour elle-même, Mme Riccoboni employait beaucoup de temps à se corriger, et se trouvait rarement satisfaite." [39] As Emily Crosby points out, if English versions of Mme Riccoboni's works were, on the whole, less successful than the originals, this was probably due to the fact that so much of this writer's appeal resided in her style and that particular quality did not always survive the translation. [40] The briefest glance at some of the English versions makes manifest the sometimes dreadful changes wrought by the translators. She was herself cognizant of the shortcomings of translations, although resigned

---

[39] J.-F. de La Harpe, *Œuvres,* XV, 524.
[40] *Une Romancière oubliée,* p. 142.

to them: to David Garrick she remarked, "Ceux qui me lisent en anglais ne connaissent ni mon style, ni ma façon de penser. C'est un inconvénient inévitable. Vraiment je suis bien pis en allemand!" (N. 59).

* * *

In some ways, Mme Riccoboni always remained a disciple of Marivaux, her first model. In this connection, it should be remembered that she was intimately familiar not only with his fiction but with his dramatic works especially; during the years when she was affiliated with the Comédie Italienne, Marivaux's plays were presented by the troupe with regularity, and Mme Riccoboni herself frequently appeared in them in the role of *seconde amoureuse*. Like Marianne and the female protagonists of these plays, Mme Riccoboni's heroines are lovely and proud, with a deep and overriding interest in affairs of the heart; they too have a penchant for extensive analysis of their every feeling. And her winsome maidens and young widows, like those in Marivaux's theatre, are wary of masculine wiles and of promises of marital bliss. There is, however, a major difference: Fanni Butlerd and her sisters are less complex and ambitious and considerably more direct than the women whom Marivaux portrays; they are far less conscious of their own charms, they do not know how to feign or disguise feelings, and they are rarely coquettish.

In most of these novels, the principle figure is a woman; she is morally strong, generous and sincere while the man against whom she is cast is hot-headed, feckless, or merely inconsiderate at best, crafty and brutal at worst. *Lettres de Fanni Butlerd*, the first of the line, is partly autobiographical. [41] In creating the novel, the author seems to have drawn on an unhappy love affair with the Comte de Maillebois [42]: she was almost certainly referring

---

[41] It is interesting to note that in a letter to Mme Riccoboni of November 27, 1758, Diderot addresses her as "Fanny" (*Correspondance*, II, 89).

[42] See, for example, J. F. Boissonade: "les *Lettres de Fanny Butler* furent réellement écrites dans une liaison avec le comte de Maillebois. Elle en était éperdument éprise, et il la quitta pour faire, sans nécessité et sans bonheur, un mariage brillant" (*Critique littéraire sous le Premier Empire*, ed. M. Naudet [Paris: Didier, 1863], II [June 21, 1811], 64).

to this incident when she wrote to Garrick, "J'ai mis dans un de mes ouvrages l'événement qui a changé les premières dispositions du sort à mon égard et sans le savoir, le public s'est vivement intéressé à des malheurs qu'il a regardés comme une fiction" (N. 78). After this success she did not hesitate to reproduce the main outlines of the story — with many variations — in her later novels. She was ever to remain the partisan of woman's rights; true love betrayed, the war between the sexes, the duplicity of man — in short, her own and Fanni's story — this is the subject matter of her novels. She continued to draw material from her own life right up to the end: her last novel, *Lettres de Milord Rivers*, contains an interpolated story about two Frenchwomen who find that friendship is preferable to love: they resemble Mme Riccoboni herself and her friend Thérèse. [43]

Each of her novels is primarily interesting not for the ideas it attempts to convey, but rather for its thoughtful and refined treatment of affairs of the heart. The author excels, largely through her artful manipulation of the letter form, at evoking the birth and gradual progress of passion, especially the moment at which the woman first perceives that love may be a disappointment. These are works of sensibility, but they are more restrained than scores of melodramatic novels which became popular following the success of *La Nouvelle Héloïse*; Mme Riccoboni, in fact, strongly disapproved of the excessive sensibility which had become the rage during the latter part of her career. [44] In *Lettres de Mylord Rivers*, published in 1776, one of the protagonists criticizes the popular novelists of the day:

> Depuis longtemps nos *très sensibles* romanciers me fatiguent. Ils veulent émouvoir, passionner, exciter des cris,

---

[43] The *Correspondance littéraire* termed this episode "très piquant," adding, "s'il est vrai, comme on nous l'assure, que ce soit une histoire véritable, et dont Mme Riccoboni et son amie Thérèse ont été elles-mêmes les héroines, ce morceau n'en est que plus précieux" (IX [October 1776], 362).

[44] In a 1772 letter to Garrick, she observed, "Nous sommes actuellement dans une fureur de *sensibilité* qui dépasse toute imagination, nos dames veulent pleurer, crier, étouffer aux spectacles.... Le sentiment est la folie du jour, on se l'est mis si fort en tête qu'il en reste bien peu dans le cœur" (N. 91).

des gémissements! Ils inventent de pitoyables malheurs, les pressent, les accumulent, en surchargent, en accablent un misérable héros, et parviennent à révolter, sans avoir trouvé le moyen d'intéresser. (XLIV)

Her own works display commendable sobriety by comparison; there are fewer tears, fewer faints and fewer accumulated misfortunes. Compared to others, they are, moreover, relatively brief and uncomplicated; the most popular were, in fact, the shortest: *Lettres de Fanni Butlerd, Histoire du Marquis de Cressy, Lettres de Juliette Catesby, Histoire d'Ernestine.* [45]

Mme Riccoboni's works began to appear at an important moment in the history of the French novel: the three noteworthy novels of Samuel Richardson had already been translated into French, but Rousseau's *Nouvelle Héloïse* would not appear for another few years. She did her best work, then, between two of the most significant figures in eighteenth-century prose fiction: while her novels are among the earliest in France to be influenced by the success of Richardson, the first three of them became best-sellers even before the publication of Rousseau's novel, so she owed virtually nothing to his influence. [46] She anticipates Rousseau in several ways: in the first place, by the epistolary form which, with *Lettres de Fanni Butlerd* and *Lettres de Juliette Catesby*, she adopted even before it became the dominant vehicle of fiction of the second half of the century, in the wake of *La Nouvelle Héloïse*; and in the second place, by the content of her novels, for as Laurent Versini points out, between *La Vie de Marianne* and *La Nouvelle Héloïse*, Mme Riccoboni and Crébillon fils are virtually the only practitioners of the "roman d'analyse." [47] Richardson's influence is visible both in the form which Mme

---

[45] The longer novels gave their creator more difficulty: of *Histoire de Miss Jenny*, the first of her novels to exceed one volume, she wrote to her editor Humblot, "Je crois avoir très mal fait d'entreprendre deux volumes: l'étendue de mon esprit se borne sans doute à un, car Mylady Catesby ne m'a point causé d'embarras" (early 1762).

[46] In fact, Mme Riccoboni had little admiration for Rousseau; in 1766 she wrote, "Rousseau cherche la célébrité, il la préfère à tout; il ne restera pas tranquille dans l'asile qu'il a désiré. N'est-il pas bien inconséquent?" (N. 24); and later the same year, "Rousseau est fou; le succès de ses ouvrages a dérangé sa tête" (N. 31).

[47] *Laclos et la tradition*, p. 41.

Riccoboni gave her novels — six of the eight are letter-novels, *Histoire d'Ernestine* and *Histoire du Marquis de Cressy* being the only exceptions — and in the fact that the principal letter-writer, as in the Richardsonian novels *Clarissa* and *Pamela*, is usually a woman, and one who is both sensitive and beleaguered. As in *Clarissa* and *Pamela*, the theme is generally the sufferings of a superior and innocent woman at the hands of a morally inferior male.

Mme Riccoboni's imitation of Richardson goes even further: the characters of four of her novels are supposed to be English [48]; in disguising her protagonists as English ladies and gentlemen, she joined the vogue of French novelists popularizing English life. In fact, she had a public not only in France but in England too, and several female English authors of the latter part of the century — including Mrs. Brooke, Mrs. Sheridan and Fanny Burney — show signs of her influence. [49] Mrs. Brooke's letter-novel, *History of Lady Julia Mandeville*, for example, bears a marked resemblance to *Lettres de Juliette Catesby* (which she had recently translated into English), although there is considerably more pathos than in the latter. [50]

Mme Riccoboni decided, after the success of her own first three novels, to attempt a translation of an English one. She chose Fielding's *Amelia*, a story rife with sentimentality; *Amélie*, which appeared in 1762, was less a translation than a loose adaptation of Fielding, as she confessed to Humblot:

> En étudiant l'anglais, sans maître, sans principes, la grammaire et le dictionnaire près de moi, ne regardant ni l'un ni l'autre, me tenant la tête à deviner, j'ai traduit tout de travers (comme j'entendais) un roman de M. Fielding. Ce qui était difficile, je le laissais là; ce que je ne comprenais point, je le trouvais mal dit: j'avançais toujours. (Early 1762)

---

[48] *Lettres de Fanni Butlerd, Lettres de Juliette Catesby, Histoire de Miss Jenny, Lettres de Mylord Rivers.*

[49] See B. G. MacCarthy, *The Female Pen* (Oxford: Cork University Press, 1946-47), vol. II: *The Later Women Novelists: 1744-1818*, pp. 66-70; and James R. Foster, *History of the Pre-Romantic Novel in England* (New York: MLA, 1949), pp. 146-47.

[50] *History of Lady Julia Mandeville* was, in fact, signed "by the translator of Lady Catesby's Letters."

Her manner of writing has nothing in common with Fielding's, and her extensive changes of the novel are an indication of her own ideas of style, her priorities and her technique. The most obvious change was the reduction of Fielding's four volumes to two; moreover, she simplified the story line considerably, diminishing the number of characters (her Mistress Elisin, for example, is a composite of two Fielding characters) and devoting fewer pages to dialogue and proportionally more to pen portraits. When Fielding copiously illustrates a person's character, Mme Riccoboni paints a brief French *portrait*. Such is the case with the dishonest Justice Thrasher, who appears early in the novel: whereas Fielding spends several paragraphs subtly and humorously evoking the "few imperfections" in his magistratical capacity, Mme Riccoboni immediately announces that Thrasher is "passablement grave, assez ignorant, très dur, et encore plus intéressé." By her sundry transformations of character and background, she gives her version a somewhat higher tone than Fielding's, systematically conferring on her characters a loftier rank, eliminating those who are too ignoble to suit her taste, suppressing all details of prison and lower class life; erotic situations become more delicate and less drawn out.[51] Not only does the hero Fenton (Fielding's Booth), become a more laudable individual, Amelia herself is made less ludicrous when Mme Riccoboni converts the infamous broken nose which Fielding gave her to an attack of illness; in Fielding, Amelia goes through life with her damaged nose, but the French translator is careful eventually to restore her heroine to full health and beauty. Part of Fielding's humor resides in his method of introducing villains in ambiguous terms, only later to reveal their unsavory character. His hero and heroine, as well as the reader, are thus continually deceived by appearances: initially they are favorably impressed by a new acquaintance, but they are frequently proved wrong by subsequent contact. Mme

---

[51] Her observations to Liston regarding *The Vicar of Wakefield* help to clarify her motivation in making such changes: "En général la pauvreté dégoûte plus qu'elle n'intéresse si on ne la présente avec une extrême délicatesse d'expression.... on voudrait donner du secours à un malheureux, mais on ne voudrait pas contempler sa misère, descendre dans le détail minutieux de ses besoins; il est un point où le dégoût l'emporte sur [la compassion]. L'histoire des prisons nous est insupportable" (N. 26).

Riccoboni makes no use of this technique. With each new character, whether he is good or bad, she provides an evaluation, and often a complete history, so that the reader is never surprised by an unexpected discovery. She makes explicit, at the first opportunity, all that Fielding only suggests. The result is that her version, while it has a charm of its own, displays considerably less humor, mystery and subtlety than the original. In the same letter to her editor in which she announces the translation, Mme Riccoboni expresses doubts about the likelihood of its enjoying much success: in any event, she quips,

> Imprimez toujours, cela deviendra ce que cela pourra. Si le livre déplaît, tant pis pour l'auteur anglais; nous dirons que cela est traduit à la lettre. Si on le lit, nous nous vanterons de l'art infini avec lequel nous avons ajouté, retranché, corrigé, embelli, notre original.

Mme Riccoboni's changes were not, on the whole, particularly felicitous and *Amélie* was not very well received. [52]

She was not discouraged, however, from trying her hand at translations. Having always admired English drama and voraciously read all the plays with which Garrick would supply her, she had even become something of an expert on the subject and at one point contemplated writing a history of the English stage. In 1768 and 1769 appeared the *Nouveau Théâtre anglais,* a collection of five English plays translated by Mme Riccoboni and Mlle Biancolelli. Included were Hugh Kelly's *False Delicacy*, George Colman's *The Jealous Wife* and *The Deuce is in Him*, Edward Moore's *The Foundling* and Arthur Murphy's *The Way to Keep Him*.

Notwithstanding her excursions into translations of English literature and her attempts to dress up her heroines and heroes as Englishmen, Mme Riccoboni's work remains essentially French. She belongs chiefly to the French tradition of the novel of analysis, and incorporates in her work none of the realistic details for which Richardson is famous. Versini suggests that Mme Ric-

---

[52] *L'Année littéraire*, for example, gave *Amélie* a tepid reception, citing "des longueurs insupportables, de mauvaises plaisanteries, des détails déplacés" (1762, IV, 174-75).

coboni represents the confluence of the English and French traditions: by form and subject matter she is English, but the fact that she is "capable de raisonner interminablement sur des sentiments et des probabilités de sentiment" demonstrates her filiation with Crébillon.[53] The taste and refinement which characterize her literary productions undoubtedly helped to establish the popularity of the epistolary novel of sentiment. The chapters which follow are an attempt to elucidate her novelistic technique, especially her handling of the epistolary form, to determine the evolution which her fiction underwent in the more than twenty years during which she wrote, and to discover, on the one hand, the originality of her ideas on love, sensibility and women, and on the other, in what ways the themes and devices wich she affects reflect the preoccupations of the era.

---

[53] *Laclos et la tradition*, p. 263.

Chapter II

NARRATION THROUGH LETTERS: TECHNICAL CONSIDERATIONS

> Ces lettres, seule consolation de mon exil, seul adoucissement de mes longs chagrins, ces lettres si chères, si souvent pressées contre mes lèvres, si souvent baignées de mes larmes, ces lettres charmantes, unique reste de mon bonheur passé, elles me disent encore que vous m'avez aimé.
>
> *Lettres de Juliette Catesby*

Like so many other fictional heroines of the mid- and late eighteenth century, the majority of Mme Riccoboni's are addicted to familiar letter-writing. This literary vogue reflects one of the real preoccupations of the era: at that time letters were a far more important means of communication than today, because people depended on the mails not only for news about friends and relatives, but also for information about the latest public developments. Much time and effort were expended in writing letters, and those received were generally saved and even circulated for the edification and admiration of friends. It was natural that under these conditions the letter-novel too should flourish. Following the success of *Lettres d'une religieuse portugaise,* published in 1669, a great many letter-novels began to appear during the last years of the seventeenth century and the beginning of the eighteenth. The form gained greatly in credibility around the middle of the eighteenth century when postal facilities were being rapidly improved and, as a consequence, the framework of the epistolary novel seemed more and more plausible.

Mme Riccoboni — like her heroine Fanni Butlerd [1] — was a devoted reader of one of the literary monuments of the preceding century: the letters of Mme de Sévigné. In addition to the inspiration found here, and to the example of two Richardsonian letter-novels, *Pamela* and *Clarissa*, three novels are important in explaining her work: *Lettres d'une religieuse portugaise*, Crébillon's *Lettres de la marquise de M*** au comte de R**** (1732) and *Lettres péruviennes* (1747) by Mme de Graffigny. Each of these novels pits a romantic heroine against a man by whom she is wronged; the women display goodness, generosity, and sincerity, while the men are inconstant and misguided at best, accomplished seducers at worst. All three novels are one-sided, bringing us the letters of the heroine alone — long and fervid epistles in which she speaks of her love and analyses her minutest feelings. Mme Riccoboni uses the genre in much the same way as these novelists: her protagonists, like those of her predecessors, are young women involved in difficult romantic situations who seek consolation in repetition and analysis of their sentiments.

The force of examples like these, however, can explain only partially why Mme Riccoboni, turning to fiction at age forty-four, espoused the letter-novel and stayed with the form over a period of twenty years. Cogent personal considerations are also at issue, relevant principally to her long and intimate connection with the theatre. Until the publication of her first novel, the chief preoccupation of Mme Riccoboni's entire adult life had been the stage, and the kind of novel which she chose to write is one which, by its very nature, is a close relative of drama. [2] In both cases, events are related by the person or persons living through them; there is no third party to mediate the action, to pass it through the prism of his own consciousness. Both of these forms place the protagonists in a privileged position vis-à-vis the public, since the characters in the epistolary novel as well as in theatre

---

[1] See *Lettres de Fanni Butlerd*, XLVI.

[2] The connection between Mme Riccoboni's theatrical and novelistic pursuits was noted as early as 1758 when Fréron, reviewing *Lettres de Juliette Catesby* in *L'Année littéraire*, wrote, "On voit bien que l'auteur connaît les règles dramatiques: les scènes sont distribuées avec art, l'attention est toujours suspendue, le dénouement se fait attendre avec impatience" (1758, VIII, 300).

appear in a sense to *be* the author, while the person whom they address becomes a stand-in for the reader or viewer. Thus arises a kind of direct contact between character and public which does not obtain in third-person reporting. In both instances, moreover, events are related *as* they occur: the hero or heroine who practices "writing to the moment," to use Richardson's expression, is similar to the stage character whom we observe living out his destiny. The result is that perspective and distance are lacking to the stage character as well as to the letter-writer: both are caught up in present circumstances and neither knows what his fate holds in store. Their words reflect the emotional involvement which they experience as they speak or write, and this in turn makes a special plea for the involvement of the theatre audience or the reader.

Both theatre and the epistolary novel call for a particular kind of character: one who displays a willingness to speak. In the third-person novel, where there is a narrator to describe and possibly to interpret the opinions and reactions of his protagonists, silence on their part is permitted. Strong and effective characters may be precisely those who say little, but whose reality is artfully impressed upon the reader by the narrator. In theatre, however, this is not the case: in a situation where characters must speak for themselves or remain unheard, where they alone can dramatize their existence, the most forceful character is often the one who speaks most cogently. This is equally true of the letter-novel which, like the theatre, presupposes on the part of the hero the desire to communicate, to proclaim his thoughts, and to reveal something of himself. Considering Mme Riccoboni's experience as an actress as well as her love of drama, it is not surprising that she chose to create fictional characters who confront the public directly, who "disent leur vie en même temps qu'ils la vivent," [3] and who show a great willingness, in fact a veritable mania, for pronouncing themselves.

If there are many similarities between the letter-novel and the theatre, there is at least one important distinction: the time sequence. Both letter and dialogue constitute an unmediated

---

[3] Jean Rousset, "Une forme littéraire: le roman par lettres" in *Forme et Signification* (Paris: José Corti, 1962), p. 67.

exchange between two persons, but in the theatre there is no time lapse between the elements of the dialogue, while the letter-novel — which is itself a kind of dialogue — involves a passage of time before the retort can be registered. This is because it is, unlike theatre, concerned with interaction between persons separated in space. Its virtue is precisely the bringing together in direct contact of such persons, and the intervals which this kind of relationship necessarily entails confer on the form its special rhythm as well as its peculiar powers and exigencies. The real reader of the letter-novel, like the audience at a play, is the contemporary of the action: he reads about it just as the writer describes it, that is to say, nearly at the moment at which it occurs. But the fictional reader — the "addressee" of the letter — does not, and thus arises the possibility of complications due to the way in which the message is transmitted. The addressee is dependent not only on the mind which composes the letter, but also on possible loss or late arrival of letters, all of which factors may affect his understanding, his reaction, and hence the outcome of events. The small amount of blank paper which separates one letter of the novel from the next is not empty space: it represents a time difference between the two letters — time which may be filled with all manner of occurrences, and which is therefore a concern of the novel.

Letter-novels may be classified in several ways — for example, according to the number of correspondents, or according to the degree to which the addressee participates in the action. [4] If the former classification is used, five of the six novels which Mme Riccoboni wrote in letter form may be described as basically of the same kind: there is only one letter-writer, who deals primarily with an addressee whose letters never appear. (This is what Laurent Versini labels the "linear formula," and what Jean Rousset calls "unilateral exchange.") This particular formula had

---

[4] Four works which discuss letter-novels and propose various methods of classifying them, and to which the present study is indebted, are Laurent Versini, *Laclos et la tradition;* Jean Rousset, *Forme et Signification;* François Jost, *Essais de littérature comparée* (Urbana: University of Illinois Press, 1968), vol. II: *Europeana;* and Vivienne Mylne, *The Eighteenth-Century French Novel* (Manchester, England: Manchester University Press, 1965).

been amply illustrated before Mme Riccoboni discovered it: *Lettres portugaises, Lettres de la marquise de M*** au comte de R***, Lettres péruviennes* are all onesided. Only the last novel which Mme Riccoboni wrote is of what Versini terms the "polyphonic" variety, where there is an actual exchange of letters among several correspondents. The full title of the novel indicates this characteristic: *Lettres de Mylord Rivers à Sir Charles Cardigan, entremêlées d'une partie de ses correspondances à Londres pendant son séjour en France.* One of the rare earlier examples of this type of epistolary novel is *Lettres persanes,* where Rica and Usbek exchange letters with each other as well as with correspondents in Persia and elsewhere. After the publication of *La Nouvelle Héloïse,* this variety of novel became more and more in evidence, finding its culmination in 1782 with *Les Liaisons dangereuses.* Only with *Lettres de Mylord Rivers* in 1777, towards the end of her literary career, did Mme Riccoboni join this trend; for the rest, she was one of a few novelists of note to continue with the linear formula even after Rousseau's success.

A second and in some ways more meaningful classification distinguishes between letter-novels in which the missives are sent to a fellow protagonist, and those in which they are addressed to a distant third party. All of Mme Riccoboni's novels except one are of the latter type: letters are a way of providing information for a friend who is geographically removed and divorced from the action. The confidant in these cases of necessity remains uninvolved, otherwise there would be no justification for filling him in on what is happening. But for this very reason, he frequently becomes little more than a letter-box and the missives themselves turn into a sort of monologue. The novel may then come very close in form to memoirs, and it is chiefly perspective which distinguishes the two: whereas the memorialist knows from the outset how it all ends, the letter-writer does not.[5]

A more complex form of the letter-novel results when the letters are sent not to an obscure outsider, but to another protagonist, as is the case in the first of Mme Riccoboni's epistolary novels, *Lettres de Mistriss Fanni Butlerd à Milord Charles Alfred*

---

[5] Many pertinent insights into letter-novel technique, including its relationship to memoirs, will be found in chapter VIII of V. Mylne, *op. cit.*

de Caitombridge ... The identity of the recipient makes all the difference: here the letter-writer communicates not just because she has something to say, but because she must say it *to a given individual*. Her motivation for writing therefore becomes a critical consideration, and her letters are no longer simply a vehicle for relating events, but are themselves events, while the composition of a letter may hold as much significance as the content — hence the greater richness of this particular form. Because Fanni Butlerd does not describe the progress of her love to a faceless friend, but actually tries to communicate that love to the man himself, the novel has an entirely different flavor from that of the other works in this author's repertoire of one-sided novels: the same story could not have been told in any form other than the epistolary.

The success or failure of an individual novel depends to a great extent on a host of concerns which are peculiar to this form and which determine the novel's credibility. Letter-novels may appear authentic only if the author is careful not to violate certain rules of verisimilitude — rules which may seem fairly obvious to the twentieth-century reader, but which were frequently disregarded by even the better novelists of the eighteenth century. Mme Riccoboni's popularity in her day is attributable, at least in part, to the fact that she understood her craft and handled her tools well.

If her protagonists write convincing letters, it is first of all because they are at ease in this medium; they are aware that writing is not speaking and that they are engaged in a kind of commerce which has demands of its own. Their concern lies not exclusively with what they say and how they say it, but also with how and when their message is to be transmitted. Because method of delivery is a frequent preoccupation among these letter-writers, the letters themselves gain in reality. Mylord Rivers, for example, often names the person to whom he is confiding his missive — even though this appellation means nothing to the real reader, since it is usually a person appearing nowhere else in the novel. But the illusion of reality is sustained because, presumably, it does mean something to the fictional reader and to Rivers himself.

It was common, when letters were such an important means of communicating, to make whole or partial copies of particularly interesting ones which had been received in order to circulate them among friends. Mme Riccoboni's heroines, like the protagonists of so many epistolary and non-epistolary novels alike (Richardson's Pamela, for example, copies out innumerable and sometimes rather lengthy letters for her parents' perusal), readily engage in the practice; the advantage, of course, is that it enables the real reader to become familiar with the contents of letters he would not otherwise see, but obviously it can also lead to excesses. The Riccoboni heroines employ a number of interesting variations which make the device seem realistic. Sophie de Vallière makes copies of important missives not only to keep her confidante informed, but also as a kind of therapy for herself; she astutely chooses a moment when she is upset and incapable of doing much else and attempts to calm herself by the mechanical task of copying documents: "Je ne puis espérer de repos, l'agitation de mon esprit éloigne le sommeil de mes yeux; pour m'arracher à moi-même, à ma triste inquiétude, je vais transcrire le manuscrit de Mylord; vous me renverrez ma copie quand vous l'aurez lue" (XLII). The request that the manuscript be returned is an interesting detail; one is led to believe that Sophie will have further uses for the document and that she is not taking such pains in copying merely for the benefit of a single person.

Another version of the procedure is found in *Lettres de Madame de Sancerre*, where the heroine, deeply affected by some letters which she has just received, writes to her friend Nancé, "Je n'ai pas la force de copier ces lettres. Le chevalier de Termes veut bien en prendre la peine. Vous les aurez de sa main" (XLI). Obviously, the hand in which a letter is written can make no difference to the real reader, but the device serves to remind him, in the first place, that these letters were truly penned by the protagonists and that Nancé would therefore be sensitive to a change in handwriting, and in the second place, that Mme de Sancerre was as human in her fatigue as anyone else. Still another variation occurs in *Lettres de Sophie de Vallière*, where Sophie sometimes remarks that, because the courier is about to depart, there is not enough time to make a copy of a letter she wishes to send on to Hortense. She is therefore obliged to include the letter itself:

> Pauline m'apporte en ce moment l'extrait qu'elle a fait des lettres de sa maîtresse. Il est bien long, il sera rempli sans doute d'inutiles détails; mais je n'ai pas le temps de le copier. Le hasard lui présente une occasion de vous envoyer très vite ce paquet, un peu gros pour la poste. (III)

Epistolary heroines frequently stopped writing because the mail was about to depart, but to use this departure as a justification for sending an unedited letter was not common. Here again, the device serves the dual purpose of convincing the reader of the intrinsic reality of all of this (there simply is not always time to make a copy, and some things are really too cumbersome to confide to the mails), and of providing him with a host of circumstances which the confidante must already know, and which, had Sophie copied out the letters, she would have been expected to suppress.

Their concern about the mails was well placed. The postal system was not always reliable and real letter-writers had constantly to face the possibility of their letters being lost or delayed in transit. The correspondence of both Diderot and Voltaire, among others, alludes repeatedly to the uncertainties of the post; in his letters to Sophie Volland, for example, Diderot speaks often of the problem and the frustrations it creates:

> Je suis désolé que cette irrégularité des postes ou de nos correspondants soit de tems en tems si cruelle pour vous. Mais, chère amie, que voulez-vous que j'y fasse? Je vous dirai comme milord d'Albermarle à Lolotte, qui admirait l'éclat d'une belle étoile: 'Ah! mon amie, ne la louez pas tant, car je ne sçaurois vous la donner.' Ah! chère amie, ne vous plaignez pas tant de la lenteur des courriers. Je ne sçaurois les faire aller plus vite.[6]

For Julie de Lespinasse, too, this was an ever-present nuisance. In one of her letters to M. de Guibert, she remarks, "Je n'entends pas pourquoi le 3 vous n'aviez pas ma lettre du 15. Je ne puis pas me faire aux irrégularités de la poste: elles font le tourment

---

[6] Diderot, *Correspondance*, III, 155 (October 18, 1750). See also Voltaire, *Correspondance*, ed. Besterman (Paris: Gallimard, 1965), II, 763 et passim.

de ma vie."[7] Like her real-life sister, Fanni Butlerd expresses continual annoyance over the vagaries of the postal system: "Vous m'avez écrit, j'en suis sûre; mais c'est ce maudit courrier qui s'amuse à se casser le cou plutôt que de m'apporter ma lettre" (LXI).

When Sophie de Vallière is on the point of changing her residence, she assures her confidante, "Mon séjour à Malzais ne ralentira point notre correspondance; j'y recevrai vos lettres deux fois la semaine" (XXX). Just as there is no real need for Mylord Rivers to identify his messengers, or for Mme de Sancerre to observe that the handwriting of a letter will not be her own, there is no apparent need for Sophie to make this observation. If she said nothing, the reader would simply assume that the correspondence would continue. The fact that she volunteers this information seems to indicate the truth of it — and, by implication, the truth of the whole novel. These little attentions to epistolary concerns, by their very superfluity as far as plot help is concerned, create an aura of authenticity.

This awareness of the realities of epistolary commerce extends to consciousness of the letter's length. Rousseau's heroes and heroines, like those of Richardson, think nothing of writing seemingly interminable letters which must fatigue both writer and reader to an exorbitant degree. Mme Riccoboni's heroines, on the whole, write letters of a more acceptable length, and on those occasions when they do become prolix, they are generally conscious of their verbosity and apologetic about it. Sophie de Vallière, for example, makes excuses for unburdening herself at the probable cost of trying the patience of her correspondent: "Mais j'abuse de vos bontés; mes longues et tristes lettres vous fatiguent. Pardonnez-moi l'ennui qu'elles vous causent. Votre tendre complaisance m'a trop accoutumée à chercher de la consolation en vous écrivant" (XXXVI).[8] But the important thing is that neither Sophie nor the other heroines transgress very

---

[7] *Lettres* (Paris: Garnier, 1921), p. 45.
[8] It might be noted that Mme Riccoboni's own letters were not usually short; those to Liston normally run to four or five pages and, in fact, she occasionally comments on their length: "Ma lettre est bien longue. Vous ajouterez, et bien *ennuyeuse*. Patience" (N. 131).

frequently in this regard: they may write often, but letters which are supposed to have been composed at one sitting are usually brief and to the point.

The defects which show up in Mme Riccoboni's technique are, for the most part, the implausibilities inherent in the epistolary genre. The most obvious of these is perhaps the unlikelihood of constant letter-writing and of recourse to the pen at the oddest moments, even in times of greatest stress: the reader must sometimes wonder if so dogged a correspondent still disposes of sufficient time to *live* the events he or she relates. The problem is apparent in letter-novels from Richardson to Rousseau; when there is but one letter-writer, moreover, as in the majority of Mme Riccoboni's works, it takes on a new dimension, for the protagonist is generally obliged to keep writing even in nearly impossible situations or the real reader cannot be informed of the story's progress.

Moreover, many things would be better described by a party other than the one involved. For instance, when Sophie writes to her friend of her intense melancholy, she begins by declaring herself too afflicted to write. It is true that the esthetic of the letter-novel, like that of the memoir-novel, assumes that people find solace in talking about their miseries, and that externalizing brings a sort of relief. In the memoir-novel, however, the character is describing the sufferings of time past, and so his willingness to speak of them is comprehensible in that they are no longer quite so immediate. But Sophie's troubles are a thing of the present: "Mes chagrins ont pris sur mon tempérament; ma santé s'altère; je ne puis dormir." She is supposedly prey to a "noire mélancolie" even as she tells of it, and that seems to involve a certain contradiction. It should be noted that the contemporary reader was probably accustomed to such distortions of verisimilitude, which were conventional in this form of fiction — just as in the memoir-novel he had to make allowances for the memorialist's unlikely powers of recollection of events long past.

Mme Riccoboni makes occasional efforts to counteract the overburdening of the main writer by providing a friend who will now and again finish out a letter, in what would otherwise be a strictly single-writer novel. This is a curious device whereby the author suddenly violates the single-writer formula in order to present the letters of a second or third writer. In *Lettres de Madame de Sancerre,* all the letters are written by Mme de Sancerre herself except for four letters and parts of a fifth, which are composed by friends of the heroine and sent to the confidant during a period when she is ill. In letter XXXIII, the heroine tells the Comte de Nancé, her correspondent, that she is not feeling well: "J'ai peine à tenir ma plume: eh, mon Dieu, qu'ai-je donc? La saison, peut-être? cet adieu qui m'a touchée... Je m'interromps... Je vous laisse. Si je suis mieux dans une heure, j'achèverai ma lettre." Mme de Sancerre does not terminate the letter, and the four which follow are written by two friends, who describe her illness to Nancé and finally announce her imminent recovery; she resumes the correspondence with letter XXXVIII. By making the two friends of Mme de Sancerre into active correspondents for a brief time, Mme Riccoboni was able to introduce the changes in point of view necessary to throw her heroine into the limelight even while she languished in a sickbed.

By this means, the central figure of the novel becomes the object of the same sort of attention as is directed toward Julie who, during portions of *La Nouvelle Héloïse,* writes no letters herself but is the focal point of all those which are written. Mme de Sancerre further resembles Julie in that she is the object of the devotion of an entire household, and is at times treated almost as though she were a saint. This is obvious from the way in which her unexpected recovery is hailed. It is her friend who evokes the reaction of the Sancerre household at the news that the mistress will live:

> Toute la maison est dans une sorte d'ivresse; ses femmes, les miennes, celles de madame de Martigues; ses gens, les nôtres, jusqu'aux moindres valets paraissent transportés de plaisir. Ils pleurent, rient, s'embrassent, se parlent et ne s'entendent point. Ils ont entouré le médecin, ils baisaient ses mains, son habit, ils l'ont presque porté dans sa voiture en le comblant de bénédictions, en le nommant un ange. En, bon Dieu, s'est écrié l'honnête vieillard, voilà une dame bien aimée, est-elle donc aussi bienfaisante qu'elle est belle? (XXXVI)

The kind of religious ecstasy with which her recovery is greeted and the veneration of which Mme de Sancerre is the object would of course be out of the question if she alone were writing: she could hardly be expected to describe such a scene herself.

A similar approach is used in *Lettres de Juliette Catesby* as well as in *Lettres de Sophie de Vallière;* in the latter novel, it serves the same end as in *Lettres de Madame de Sancerre*. When the heroine is so deeply affected by events that for her to describe them in writing would be either impossible or dangerous for her health, the pen is taken up by friends who inform her confidante of the progress of Sophie's affairs. Thus, the last letter of the novel, containing details of the heroine's unexpected good fortune and impending marriage, is written to the confidante by a friend, Mme de Monglas, who explains, "Si elle vous écrivait à présent, les détails où elle entrerait augmenterait peut-être cette espèce de trouble, d'émotion dont on craint les suites" (XLIV). The fact that Sophie suspends her writing at the novel's conclusion is, moreover, symbolic, for Sophie's marriage confers on her a husband and companion at the same time as a new status in society: she is no longer the lonely orphan, deprived of social recognition, whose sole consolation and pastime is writing letters.

Another variant is found in *Juliette Catesby;* the last letter of this novel has a rather unique character, being a sort of communal effort, with Juliette, Ossery (her new husband) and a lady friend all making contributions to its composition. It is written partly by husband and friend not because Juliette is somehow incapacitated like Mme de Sancerre or Sophie, but because of the exceptionally joyous event which this letter announces: the wedding of Juliette and Ossery. The latter begins the communication and after about a page of prose declares, "hier fut le jour à jamais fortuné." At this point, his wife of one day seizes the pen to exclaim, "Eh bien, cet indiscret, il ne me laissera rien à vous dire." She continues for a few lines only to have the friend pluck it from her as she is in the middle of a sentence. Juliette eventually manages to retrieve the right of composition and finishes the letter with an invitation to her confidante to come and see for herself. Here the very form of the letter captures something of the excitement and confusion of the occasion, and at the same time allows the reader a brief first-hand glimpse of the male protagonist at the end of the novel, when all the difficulties have been resolved and he and the heroine have been married. Only at this moment — when Ossery has been forgiven for a previous infidelity to Juliette and his redemption is assured — is the ultimate reality conferred on him: that of having his own words presented directly, rather than being quoted by Juliette. Ossery is incorporated into Juliette's correspondence as into her life. (Alfred, the lover who is rejected at the end of *Lettres de Fanni Butlerd,* at no point enjoys the same distinction: his own letters never appear except in the brief quotations Fanni chooses to give, and he remains throughout a more shadowy, less comprehensible figure than Ossery.)

In spite of the fact that Mme Riccoboni occasionally relieves the main letter-writer in the manner described, the central figure in these novels is still faced with a task of enormous dimensions, for epistolary heroes and heroines must sometimes write when ordinary humans would find it impossible. Like a number of other heroines who miraculously find the energy to compose lengthy letters at death's door, Fanni Butlerd has strength enough to write when she is dangerously ill. She takes pains to apprise her reader of the courage which this involves, however, heading one of her letters "Lundi, dans mon lit, malade comme un chien" (XXIII). At another moment, she rather self-consciously announces, "C'est après sept heures des plus violentes douleurs, que je trouve dans mon cœur la force de vous écrire, malgré l'abattement de toute la machine" (LXXV). Juliette Catesby may be on the point of succumbing to the emotion caused by the receipt of a letter, but she all the same musters the energy to transcribe it immediately for her confidante: "Ah, comment vous dire, vous exprimer! Aurais-je la force d'écrire?" (XXVIII). One supposes, and with reason, that she will manage.

If a heroine is to share with her reader every thought and experience at the very moment when they occur, then she must write not only when physically or emotionally incapacitated, but also under some strange external conditions. Neither time, nor place, nor the lack of writing materials deters the eighteenth-century fictional hero or heroine who has something to say. Saint-Preux, in *La Nouvelle Héloïse,* for example, composes a love letter while he is crouched in Julie's dressing-room and awaiting their nocturnal rendez-vous, while Valmont of *Les Liaisons dangereuses* derives ironic satisfaction from using one of his paramours as a writing table. And Richardson's Clarissa, locked in an almost barren room by her irate family, somehow succeeds in smuggling in pen and paper so that she may write to Anna Howe. Several of Mme Riccoboni's heroines have the annoying habit of writing while visitors are present and when they should be speaking or listening. Some of the most striking instances of this occur in *Lettres de Juliette Catesby,* where the heroine can rarely tear herself away from her correspondence long enough to be civil to her numerous unsolicited suitors: "Voilà le maussade personnage établi dans mon cabinet; insensiblement il gagne du terrain; il est près, tout près de moi... il lit presque ce que j'écris... je voudrais qu'il le lût pour lui apprendre... je continue exprès..." (VIII). And Mme de Sancerre, when friends pay a surprise visit as she is composing a letter, rhetorically asks her confidant, "Que disent-ils?" before she actually lays her pen aside and gives them her whole attention (XLI).

Juliette Catesby is so inveterate a correspondent that she is sometimes loathe to interrupt this activity even long enough to read her mail. At one point, upon receiving a letter from her estranged lover, she is so troubled that, instead of reading it — which would be the obvious course of action — she composes a long letter to Henriette, her confidante, which begins,

> Ah, grand Dieu, quelle émotion! quelle surprise! Sous une enveloppe dont la main m'est inconnue, une lettre de mylord d'Ossery... oui, de lui, en vérité... voilà son caractère... elle est de lui... Mon Dieu, elle est bien de lui!... D'où vient-elle?... qui l'a apportée?... comment?... pourquoi?... Il m'écrit encore!... à moi! ... que me veut-il? ma main tremble. (XX)

She continues to wonder, while composing an entire page, what Ossery could want of her, at one time exclaiming "je ne puis écrire" as she goes on writing. Subsequent notes from Ossery elicit equally unrealistic behavior; even when she takes the time to read them, Juliette will sometimes provide, Pamela-like, a running commentary on the delivery and the opening pages:

> Mais on m'annonce Abraham, le valet-de-chambre de Mylord... Mon Dieu, que me veut-il? Oh, le cœur me bat... C'est un billet qu'il m'apporte... ce pauvre

> Abraham, il est si charmé de me revoir qu'il ne peut parler... Mais lisons... ces lignes sont tracées avec difficulté... Il a été bien mal... (XXX)

It is no wonder that poor Abraham should find it difficult to speak, confronted as he is with Juliette's refusal to stop emoting and writing long enough to give him a hearing. This is a common device among novelists, Richardson and others, and the kind of thing which Fielding ridicules in *Shamela*. It is at times like these that the esthetic of "writing to the moment" becomes absurd.

For most authors of letter-novels, and for the dramatist as well, exposition poses a problem. In one way or another, the audience must be made aware of what is going on, yet the characters in the novel or on the stage should not tell each other things which they already know. Letter-writers and characters in a play alike sometimes do resort to repeating things of which their addressee or listener does not need to be reminded. They may try to disguise the absurdity of the procedure by prefacing their remarks with a "vous savez que." The long memoir of Miss Jenny to the Comtesse de Roscomonde is of this type:

> Vous n'avez point oublié, Madame, l'aimable Sara Alderson. Vous étiez en Irlande quand elle mourut. Vous pleurâtes la compagne de votre enfance, son souvenir vit encore dans le cœur d'une amie. La ressemblance de mes traits avec les siens vous donna le désir de former, d'entretenir cette liaison qui m'est devenue si chère. (Part I, pp. 5-6)

If Jenny realizes that the Countess has not forgotten, then why speak of it? It is only too clear that the real reader and not the Comtesse de Roscomonde is intended to benefit from the reminder. Again later in the same novel, Jenny relates a number of details with which her correspondent is already familiar:

> Surprise et charmée en voyant le portrait de Lady Alderson dans mon cabinet, vous le considérâtes longtemps; vous ne pouviez détourner vos regards de cet agréable tableau. Croyant que je le tenais du hasard, vóus me le demandâtes. (Part IV, pp. 25-26)

Here the abuse is at its worst, because Jenny is telling her friend not simply things which the latter already knows, but things which the Countess herself did, thought, and communicated to Jenny.

Without a narrator to assist them, fictional letter-writers not only provide the public with factual information, they also express their own emotional states. This is equally incumbent on the stage character, but he disposes of any number of means for conveying them; a gesture or an inflection of the voice may alert the audience to his distress or joy. He can hesitate and space his remarks so that sighs may fill the intervals between words. Mme Riccoboni's protagonists, like so many other eighteenth-century heroes and heroines, attempt to express a whole gamut of emotions by means of a parallel device which is nevertheless totally implausible in this context: the suspended sentence. At those moments when, were she on stage, she would hesitate, a letter-writer uses an artificial means to indicate that hesitation and records three dots. Thus does Juliette Catesby attempt to render her distress at meeting her former lover after a long separation: "quel trouble dans mon âme... je l'ai vu... il m'a parlé... lui-même... il était au bal... oui lui... Mylord d'Ossery" (XXXIV). The suspended utterance is less than satisfactory here: as an imitative device for speech, it is inappropriate in a letter-novel, where the character is supposedly writing and not speaking. In third-party reporting, it may indicate the reluctance or trouble which the narrator *observes* in the person speaking and which he *transcribes* in this conventional manner; as a stage direction, it may be used in a similar way. When the speaker himself, on the other hand, resorts to recording his speech in a disjointed style, it indicates a self-consciousness on his part which betrays the claims to authenticity which the novel might otherwise make. Not only is Juliette Catesby distressingly aware of her own hesitations in communicating, but she is transcribing them by means of a dramatic convention in what are supposed to be real letters. Mme Riccoboni, like other authors of epistolary novels, attempts to use the suspended utterance for dramatic effect *in and of itself*, and such a usage is patently fictitious.

Another major difficulty of the one-sided letter-novel which shows up, for example, in Crébillon's *Lettres de la marquise* and Mme de Graffigny's *Lettres péruviennes*, is the narrowness of the focus — what one might call "tunnel vision." The reader can experience events only as they are witnessed by a single writer; he cannot get beyond that writer to view him and the world about him as others do. In some cases, this can entail the difficulty of knowing how far to trust the writer. In *Les Liaisons dangereuses*, some of the writers tell outright lies or, at best, half truths; the reader knows this because he can compare differing versions of the same event written by two different people, or by the same person to two different addressees. Thus he is permitted a more complete view of reality, while at the same time he can judge which protagonists are guilty of insincerity or self-deception. In the single-writer novel, no such control is normally possible; we are for the most part limited to reading what one person writes to one other person.

One of the means which Mme Riccoboni does use in order to broaden the focus somewhat is the quotation; protagonists frequently scatter throughout their letters italicized words, sentences and even entire paragraphs which represent excerpts from their friends' letters, especially those of the confidant with whom they are corresponding and whose letters do not themselves appear. This technique has the advantage of providing another viewpoint and, in addition, making it clear that a real exchange is taking place, even though we see only half of it. In *Lettres de Sophie de Vallière*, the first letter of Sophie to Hortense begins with a number of italicized words which are presumably quotations from a letter which Sophie has just received: "Mon silence vous *inquiète*, vous *alarme*, vous *afflige*." But the method is in some novels used too often and with too little discretion not to create an annoyance for the reader. Sophie's letters are sometimes little more than lengthy quotations from Hortense's, with a minimum of commentary. They frequently begin with a six- or seven-line excerpt, into which Sophie intersperses only a "dites-vous" of her own. The beginning of letter XI is typical; Sophie tells Hortense what the latter has just written to her:

> Vous ne *concevez* pas mon *inquiétude* sur les *assiduités du marquis de Germeuil, elles vous paraissent la suite naturelle d'une intimité formée dès nos plus jeunes ans,* entretenue par *une conformité remarquable dans nos goûts, et dans nos sentiments.*

Mme de Sancerre too does this in her letters to the Comte de Nancé:

> Vous êtes *surpris, très surpris,* de quelques expressions de mes lettres; plus *surpris* encore de m'entendre dire en parlant de madame de Montalais: *mon sort a été bien différent du sien. Aucun mari,* pensez-vous, *n'eut de plus tendres égards pour sa femme que le comte de Sancerre.* (VIII) [9]

Probably neither Hortense nor Nancé requires the exact replay of everything which he has recently written. The objective, clearly, is to provide us with an opinion contrasting with that of the heroine, but the method is somewhat facile. Hortense's impressions, like Nancé's, might better have been worked into her friend's letters instead of appearing in undigested form.

A final area which posed a certain amount of difficulty for Mme Riccoboni, and which she sometimes treated in such a way as to weaken verisimilitude, is that of time and chronology. Throughout the eighteenth century, fictional handling of these matters tended to be imprecise and impressionistic, and they created a special problem for the author of a letter-novel which, by its very nature, is closely tied to concerns of time. Because lapses in time are often charged with possible meaning, it is essential that the reader have some notion of the rapidity with which one letter follows another. Most eighteenth-century epistolary authors, nevertheless — Rousseau, for instance — give no indication of dates. One of the strengths of *Les Liaisons dangereuses,* by contrast, is in the precise dating of the letters (Montesquieu, too, indicates dates in the *Lettres persanes,* though ostensibly according to the Persian calendar). Only in her two earliest letter-novels, *Lettres de Fanni Butlerd* and *Lettres de Juliette Catesby,* does Mme Riccoboni do so. Both of these cite the day of the week when the letter was written and Juliette also

---

[9] Mme Riccoboni's own letters to Liston are similar in this regard. She writes, for example, "Mon cher Liston ne *m'oubliera jamais?* Il désire *revoir son amie?* Passer un *longtemps avec elle?*" (N. 61). And again, "Vous avez du *plaisir* à *lire mes lettres.* Vous m'écrivez *sans peine,* vous *m'aimez* plus que *jamais*" (N. 66).

specifies the place of composition — for example "Lundi à Erford" or "Samedi à Vinchester" — while Fanni sometimes notes the time of day and adds "dans mon lit" or "au coin du feu." Perhaps one can explain these exceptions by the fact that the three subsequent single-writer letter-novels contain more interpolated stories of sometimes considerable length, and what matters in them is not so much when or how a letter was composed as what it relates. While in the early works, then, the fact of writing is significant in itself, in the later linear novels, letters are sometimes important less as testimonies to the emotional vicissitudes of the heroine than as documents regarding her many adventures and mishaps.

In the novels where dates are not supplied, there are occasionally some rather shocking discoveries for the reader. For example, at the beginning of letter VII of *Lettres de Sophie de Vallière*, the heroine writes: "Après un mois passé sans vous écrire, je puis donner moi-même des preuves de ma douloureuse existence." The reader, who had no way of guessing that the end of letter VI was the prelude to a long silence, is surprised that the tiny blank separating these two letters represents a lapse of one month, whereas elsewhere it means only a day or two, or even a few hours. The difficulty resides in the single-writer technique; Sophie indicated failing health in letter VI, but unlike Mme de Sancerre, she has no friends about her at that moment to tell the public that she has in fact been brought down by it. Either Sophie must write when she is too ill to do so, or the reader can know of her plight only when it has been resolved and she can again correspond. At that point, however, it is indeed a shock and, moreover, no longer a very relevant one since Sophie has passed the crisis. A parallel problem occurs at the beginning of one of the missives in *Lettres de Madame de Sancerre*, where the heroine says that she is glad that her correspondent has finally answered her last letter, since a month has elapsed since she sent it. Here again, the reader is caught off guard, having initially assumed that this letter, like the others, followed the previous one at an interval of only a few days.

In *Lettres de Mylord Rivers*, the only Riccoboni novel where the letters of more than one correspondent regularly appear, the author manifests no concern whatever for time. Often a letter is immediately followed by the response which it elicits, even though a courier must have twice crossed the English Channel in order for this to occur. The responses seem to come too quickly; for example, letter XXXVI from Adeline to Mylord Rivers is answered by letter XXXVII — even though she is at home in England and he traveling in France. Laclos will perfect the technique in this regard by interspersing between a letter and its rejoinder one or several messages written by or to different parties; thus, when the answer to an earlier message appears, the reader has the artificial impression that an appropriate amount of time has elapsed for the addressee to have received the letter and replied to it.

Technical defects are sometimes apparent in the novels of Mme Riccoboni but, on the whole, she handles her tools well; while she does fall victim to some of the commoner, more grievous faults which plagued the writers of the period, her novels are nonetheless more believable than many. There are no absurdities to compare, for example, with Mme de Graffigny's Peruvian princess who supposedly expresses extremely nuanced thought by means of knotting colored cords and who, after only six months in France, is sufficiently in control of the language to translate her letters into perfect French. Mme Riccoboni's letters are nearly always adequately motivated and are, for the most part, composed under realistic conditions; they are usually short and to the point, with none of the lengthy, gratuitous and often tiresome digressions which appear in so many of the novels of her contemporaries.

If the technique of the eighteenth-century letter-novel appears deficient, it should be remembered that the genre in this period was still unsettled. The effort to provide the public with the aura of authenticity which it desired placed on the writer certain constraints which he had not experienced before, and solutions to sundry technical problems came only gradually. Laclos would eventually elaborate a nearly flawless technique to support a remarkably convincing novel: his correspondents compose carefully motivated letters of reasonable length, and usually do so under credible circumstances. The letters are, moreover, brilliantly orchestrated and the exchange of letters is an important factor in the plot. But Laclos' novel appeared only in 1782 — twenty-five years after the publication of Mme Riccoboni's first epistolary novel, *Lettres de Fanni Butlerd;* it came, then, not at the beginning, but almost at the end of a century-long tradition in the novel.

Chapter III

THE LETTER'S MANY MEANINGS: *FANNI BUTLERD*

> J'écris vite, je ne saurais rêver à ce que je veux dire; ma plume court, elle suit ma fantaisie: mon style est tendre quelquefois, tantôt badin, tantôt grave, triste même, souvent ennuyeux, toujours vrai.
>
> *Lettres de Fanni Butlerd*

The first of Mme Riccoboni's novels, *Lettres de Mistriss Fanni Butlerd,* published in 1757, is also her finest. It was an instant success. Aimed at a public which exacted an appearance of authenticity, the work purported to be a translation from the English: the title page announces that the letters were "écrites en 1735, traduites de l'anglais en 1756 par Adélaïde de Varançai." Such was the air of sincerity and genuineness of Fanni's letters that the novel was generally taken for a true correspondence with the Comte de Maillebois, with whom Mme Riccoboni seems to have had an unfortunate love affair. This was the reaction of Grimm in the *Correspondance littéraire:*

> Ce sont des lettres d'une femme à son amant, qui n'ont jamais existé en anglais. Elles ont été écrites très réellement, non pour le public mais pour un amant chéri, et on le voit bien par la chaleur, le désordre, la folie, le naturel et le tour original qui y règnent.... Malgré cet effort de déguiser et d'ôter la touche de la vérité, vous y trouverez des lettres qui vous feront le plus grand plaisir du monde.[1]

---

[1] III (April 1757), pp. 365-66.

While Grimm promptly discounted the novel's claims to being a translation, he was prepared to grant it this more important kind of authenticity because of its warmth, naturalness and unstudied eloquence. *Lettres de Fanni Butlerd* is distinct among the author's works in that it displays a unity of form and content which she never duplicated. Fanni's correspondence and her drama are so intimately related that neither could exist without the other. The epistolary technique is inherent in the novel because the letters *are* the story: they constitute not simply the external form of the novel, but turn out to be to a large extent its very subject matter as well. If this is so, it is because the addressee of Fanni's letters is not an obscure confidant whose connection with the plot is tenuous at best, but rather the man with whom she is in love and who is therefore her major preoccupation.

One of the greatest merits of *Lettres de Fanni Butlerd* is the simplicity of plot, and because of this characteristic, the epistolary form is particularly well suited to the novel: in the almost total absence of action, letter-writing is what matters most of all. *Lettres de Fanni Butlerd* concerns but two people: an ardently honest woman is pitted against a fickle and deceitful man and the novel recounts the heroine's emotional vicissitudes and her gradual discovery of the man's character. Unlike some of the later Riccoboni novels, where there occur extraordinary adventures, chance encounters, deaths, disguises and rapes, this novel contains almost no secondary characters, no subplots, no interpolated stories or letters. It is the story of one episode in the life of a woman about whom the reader knows only that she is not exceedingly wealthy, that she has a friend named Miss Betzi, a sister whom she finds tedious, and that she had a brother who died. The setting too is dim; all realistic detail is suppressed and there is little sense of place, color or dress.

In one vital respect, however — chronology — this novel is more definite than those which followed by the same author. The precision of *Lettres de Fanni Butlerd* is, in this regard, in striking contrast to one of its models, Crébillon's *Lettres de la marquise*. As Vivienne Mylne observes, one of the flaws of Crébillon's novel is the lack of exactness with respect to dates; it is impossible to know how long the Marquise's affair lasted, and whether she required days, weeks, or even months to fall in love and to become the Count's mistress.[2] In *Lettres de Fanni Butlerd,* on the other hand, where the heroine indicates the day of the week when she writes each letter, the reader can, with a little effort, closely determine the duration of the romance and the amount of time separating one crucial occurrence from the next.

Fanni Butlerd consists of 116 letters which are written over a period of approximately thirty-three weeks. It may be divided into three parts: the interval before the love affair begins, the time during which the lover is absent, and the period after he returns. The first thirty-six letters, which cover a span of nine weeks, describe Alfred's gradual seduction of Fanni, who readily admits her love for him but remains reluctant to become his mistress — leaving herself, however, open to persuasion. Two weeks after she succumbs (an event noted in letter XXXVI), Alfred leaves London to serve with the military; he is gone for about six weeks, during which time Fanni composes letters XLIII through LXXXIX. After Alfred's return come the revelation of his impending marriage to someone else and the end of the romance. This third and last section of the novel is temporally the longest, lasting perhaps sixteen weeks, but is marked by the smallest number of letters (twenty-six) — which is itself indicative of the breakdown of the affair.[3] In fact, Mme Riccoboni evidently felt compelled somehow to justify the continuation of the correspondence beyond Alfred's return, since at this point it is no longer necessary that the lovers exchange letters. The reason which Fanni advances for continuing to write is not entirely felicitous: "Vous aimez mes lettres; vous ne voulez point que votre retour vous prive du plaisir d'en recevoir. Celle que vous m'écrivez est charmante; en demandant ainsi, mon cher Alfred, on est bien sûr d'obtenir" (XC). Here the scaffolding of the letter-

---

[2] *The Eighteenth-Century French Novel* (Manchester: University Press, 1965), p. 161.

[3] David L. Anderson points out that "Almost without exception, the last group of letters in the novel (XC-CXVI) omit any mention of time, stating only the day the letter was written. Fanni's role as a victim is thus supported structurally within the form of the novel by the reflection of her feelings in her ability (or inability) to relate to concrete reality, i. e., the time of day." ("Abélard and Héloïse: eighteenth-century motif," *Studies on Voltaire and the Eighteenth Century,* 84 [1971], 41.)

novel shows: not only does the reason seem artificial (especially since the reader already suspects that Alfred is less than completely devoted to Fanni), but Alfred hardly needs to be told what he has just asked.

During the time covered by the 116 letters of the novel, very little happens. Yet a situation which by its essential sameness might be overwhelmingly tedious, is here highly charged because of the emotion which the heroine brings to it and the skill with which her feelings are conveyed. The letters are structured so that they are never boring, and although they all say much the same thing, they say it in different ways and rarely seem repetitive. The novel has a lively start with a succession of brief letters which adeptly present Fanni's predicament; from then on, somewhat longer and more passionate letters alternate with terse notes which embody now an outcry and now a sigh. The mood is never the same for long and its expression too is greatly varied: Fanni exults, broods, flirts and teases in rapid succession. While in one letter she may pronounce herself the most fortunate of women, in the next she may declare, "Jamais ennui ne fut comparable à celui que je sens; si j'avais pu le prévoir, je n'aurais point aimé" (LXIX). To this novel one might apply what Vivienne Mylne writes in explaining the charm of *Lettres de la marquise:* within the limits of a basic situation, the tone shifts "from the serious to the frivolous, from annoyance to teasing, from the unequivocal to a hint of uncertainty." [4]

The tender, lyrical outpourings which Fanni addresses to her lover during the greater part of the novel place this work in the tradition of *Lettres portugaises* and make these the only true love letters in Mme Riccoboni's novels. Only Fanni's letters are presented, but the novel assumes that a real and virtually uninterrupted exchange of letters is taking place, and in this respect it resembles *Lettres de la marquise,* which also detail a woman's seduction and abandonment by a man who writes to her continually but whose letters are not made available to the public.

This particular formula results in the preeminence of the heroine, since all the action is presented through her eyes and

---

[4] *The Eighteenth-Century French Novel*, p. 158.

from the feminine point of view. The reader, who is allowed access to only half the correspondence, is always kept somewhat in the dark, never enjoying full knowledge of events, nor complete understanding of the man's behavior. He has, therefore, the impression of a partially veiled reality. In *Lettres de Fanni Butlerd,* this aura of uncertainty is reinforced by means of half-explained allusions to things which the lover has done or said in his letters; the heroine presents these items obliquely, often considering them only long enough to record her reaction. The opening lines of the first letter which Fanni writes provide a good example of the technique: "Après avoir bien réfléchi sur votre songe, je vous félicite, Milord, de cette vivacité d'imagination qui vous fait rêver de si jolies choses: ménagez ce bien; une douce erreur forme tout l'agrément de notre vie." The reader suspects that Alfred has dreamed of some possible future relationship between himself and Fanni, but this is never explicitly stated. For the remainder of the novel, the reader is allowed only this sort of fleeting glimpse of Alfred's words and actions. Most important, he can never be sure of what Alfred really thinks or wants. But in spite of the mystery surrounding the male figure, his presence is forceful and noticeable at every moment of the correspondence; as Jean Rousset writes of *Lettres portugaises* and *Lettres de la marquise,*

> le destinataire absent y est présent de tout son poids, la correspondance entière est suspendue à son comportement invisible; ce personnage silencieux n'est pas un figurant, il est un personnage du roman. Cette présence constante du destinataire à l'horizon change le monologue en dialogue, la confession en action, et modifie profondément la conscience que l'on prend de soi-même aussi bien que la manière dont on se communique.[5]

Alfred is in this sense a very real force in the novel, since it is love for him which moves Fanni to write, and the desire to affect him in one way or another which may determine what and how she writes. Moreover, it is not just Fanni's writing which advances

---

[5] *Forme et Signification,* p. 72.

the plot, but the fashion in which Alfred reads and interprets what she says.

In *Lettres de Fanni Butlerd,* in short, the epistolary technique is at the heart of the novel because it serves to do more than convey the story: it is the means by which psychology is created. The act of writing is an element in the plot, and the sending and receiving of letters is important in determining the fate of the main protagonist. Letters do not merely serve to describe feelings and events; they are intimately concerned with why a person feels as he does and with why events take the turn they do. The psychology of the letter and the implications of corresponding are more highly developed here than in any other novel of Mme Riccoboni, and this fact contributes significantly to its superiority. Fanni Butlerd is distinct from her sister heroines precisely because she writes to her lover; in the last analysis, this is a novel about letters and what it means to write and receive them.

* * *

The exchange of letters plays two distinct roles in Fanni's relationship with Lord Alfred, corresponding to the periods before and after he has seduced her. During the first, letters are principally an aid to the seducer, while during the second they function mainly as a crutch for the woman. Fanni's first thirty-six letters, written before she consents to have an affair with Alfred, are somewhat more contentious than the later ones. Having admitted that she loves him, she strives frantically to resist his pressures, while he avails himself of every possible argument to convince her. While Fanni maintains that an admission of her feelings constitutes in itself more of a commitment than Alfred has the right to expect, he accuses her of loving him imperfectly because the only assurances which she is willing to give are verbal. This, his main line of attack, is one to which Fanni, who prides herself on the depth of her feelings, is only too susceptible. [6]

---

[6] Mme Riccoboni was herself sensitive to the suggestion that her friends' affection for her was greater than her own for them; to Garrick she wrote, "Vous croyez m'aimer plus que je ne vous aime? Une personne vaine serait peut-être flattée de vous laisser cette idée, mais une âme sensible en est blessée" (N. 47).

She attempts to counter his arguments by evoking the dangers of a love affair for the sensitive woman, but this device actually works against her in the long run, thereby illustrating a remark of the hero of Duclos' *Confessions du comte de* ***: "Une femme qui parle souvent des dangers de l'amour s'aguerrit sur les risques, et s'y familiarise avec la passion; c'est toujours parler de l'amour, et l'on n'en parle guère impunément." [7] By dint of writing that she must never give in, Fanni accustoms herself to thinking that some day she might. In effect, it soon becomes clear that the battle is all the more unequal because Fanni is defending herself not only against Alfred but also against an even more formidable adversary — her own deep yearnings to love him. Alfred, moreover, can hardly ignore the factors which are operating in his favor when he reads a letter like the following, in which Fanni allows the attraction she feels to become manifest:

> Je songe à ce merveilleux anneau dont on a tant parlé ce soir: on me le donne, je l'ai, je le mets à mon doigt, je suis invisible, je pars, j'arrive... où? devinez... dans votre chambre: j'attends votre retour, j'assiste à votre toilette de nuit, même à votre coucher. Cela n'est pas dans l'exacte décence; mais je suppose que Milord est modeste. (XXV)

The reverie becomes more and more erotic until finally, evoking "le silence, la nuit, l'amour," Fanni cuts herself short with "vite, qu'on m'ôte l'anneau. Bon Dieu, où m'allait-il conduire?" [8]

Here and elsewhere Fanni tends to disregard rules of decency and propriety when she has pen in hand (a neglect which sets her off from the other Riccoboni heroines, who remain at all

---

[7] In *Romanciers du XVIIIe siècle*, ed. Étiemble (Paris: Gallimard, 1965), II, 280.

[8] In a letter to Garrick written twelve years after the publication of *Fanni Butlerd*, the author describes a similar fantasy: "Si j'avais une baguette de fée je m'en servirais pour vous fixer près de votre table quand vous m'écrivez; j'arrêterais la rapidité de cette plume légère, qui court, vole et laisse à peine sur le papier des traces de son passage — eh, que je suis bête! Si je la possédais, cette baguette, j'irais vous voir, vous embrasser, causer avec vous" (N. 50). She alludes to the "baguette de fée" again in a 1771 letter to Liston (N. 69).

times decorous).[9] The very fact that Fanni, while outwardly refusing Alfred's demands, simultaneously writes letters so revealing and provocative, is an indication of how the seduction is actually accomplished by means of letters. She would never *speak* to Alfred in terms as familiar and suggestive as these, but she has less control over herself when writing than when speaking, because the dangers of writing — thanks to distance — seem lesser. In this respect she resembles that other famous epistolary heroine, Mme de Tourvel, whose seduction is also effected largely by means of correspondence. "Les femmes en écrivant se laissent aller, donnent des armes contre elles, se familiarisent avec les passions tendres, et sont presque toujours faibles la plume à la main," explains Dorat in *Les Malheurs de l'inconstance*.[10]

Letters are dangerous in that they almost inevitably lead a woman to reveal more of herself than she had intended; but the perils of an epistolary commerce do not lie simply in the fact that one's defenses are down when one writes: feelings may in fact be fostered or even brought into existence by the very act of describing them on paper. The letter wields an extraordinary creative power: a character who sets out to articulate in writing what she is undergoing, may well end up experiencing an emotion by reason of evoking it. The composition of a letter is in itself an experience as critical for the writer as any other, and the decisive moment in the evolution of her feelings may be the one in which she transposes them on paper. Furthermore, the more often she attempts to describe her feelings, and the more carefully she endeavors to render them in the terms and style which a conventional letter demands, the more they are likely to become a part of

---

[9] Fréron disapproved of the novel in part for these very reasons; Fanni's language he found "bassement familier" and the heroine herself imprudent and indecent: "Elle se livre sans retenue à toute la vivacité de sa passion; elle s'en explique sans gêne avec celui qui en est l'objet" (*L'Année littéraire*, 1757, VI, 52-59).

[10] Paris: Delalain, 1772, p. 127, quoted in *Laclos et la Tradition*, p. 161. Sophie de Vallière is another Riccoboni heroine who illustrates Dorat's remark; she laments ever having given her suitor the upper hand by writing to him: "Une basse complaisance pour moi-même ... m'a conduite à entretenir un commerce qu'il fallait rompre: l'intérêt ne m'a point séduite, l'ambition ne m'a point éblouie; j'ai refusé de grands avantages, et je n'ai pu me priver d'une dangereuse correspondance. Ah! je voudrais n'avoir jamais écrit à Monsieur de Germeuil" (XXXVI).

her.[11] This consideration is essential to an understanding not just of the psychology of Fanni Butlerd, but even of the other Riccoboni heroines who are such inveterate correspondents: their emotions may stem in some measure from the attempt to put them down on paper (this is more true of writing than of speaking for the former is a more considered enterprise), while their descriptions of an emotional state are in turn dependent to some degree on the words, phrases and letter style which are at their disposal.

While Fanni helps to bring about her downfall by the letters she writes, those which she receives and consents to read are also important factors: just as a woman's defenses are weak while she is writing, so are they weak when she is reading. She is less able to protect herself against a man's letters than against his spoken words — letters being more insidious since a woman tends to allow herself to read things to which her education has conditioned her to refuse to listen. When once a man succeeds in having his letters read, the battle is half won. Not only is the woman unprepared to react decisively and unhesitatingly to defend herself against the written word (as she would against the spoken), but, as Versini points out, "Une lettre demeure, on la garde malgré soi, on la relit."[12] This is crucial: since it was common practice to keep and reread letters (Mme de Tourvel in *Les Liaisons dangereuses* will even make copies of letters which decency obliges her to return to Valmont), they may exert a much stronger influence than words which, once pronounced, vanish. The tendency to reread seems to be congenital with Fanni Butlerd: in her second letter, she writes, "J'ai lu deux fois votre billet, et j'allais le lire une troisième, quand je me suis demandé la raison de ce goût pour la lecture." As she becomes more and more involved, she tends more and more to reread, and the number of readings she accords to a given letter escalates. In letter XII, she writes that, finding herself unable to sleep, "Je prends un livre, je le laisse; c'est votre lettre que je lis; je la finis, je la recommence: je voudrais l'oublier, pour la relire encore." Fanni

---

[11] A character in *Histoire de Miss Jenny* says in regard to a love affair she had, "Seules interprètes de nos sentiments, des lettres passionnées en augmentaient la vivacité" (part III, p. 63).

[12] *Laclos et la Tradition*, p. 161.

continues to struggle, to insist that it is undesirable, unwise, and, in fact, impossible to begin a love affair, but she is already lost. By reading and rereading, by engaging in so much discussion as to the advisability of an affair, she has signed the warrant for her own seduction. While she flounders, the inevitable occurs.

Once she has succumbed, letters begin to play a different role in her life: they are no longer the tools of the seducer, but rather the means by which Fanni is able to fulfill a pressing need of her own. In the same letter where the reader learns that Fanni has become Alfred's mistress, he finds an indication of the new significance of the letter. Remarking on the absolute necessity of their correspondence to her equilibrium, and on the power of the epistle to create misery or happiness, Fanni declares: "Cette lettre que j'attends, que je désire, va détruire ou confirmer ma joie.... Mon Dieu, si un peu moins de vivacité dans votre style... s'il vous échappait... si une seule expression me faisait craindre..." (XXXVI). Her immediate and continual fear is that his letters will prove him unworthy or unappreciative of the sacrifice which she has made; her hope is that the ardor with which he writes will demonstrate that she was right in giving herself to him. In either case, it is the letter which holds the key to her fate. Since, in Fanni's own mind, Alfred's love is not entirely sure, and the relationship not completely satisfactory, she continually looks for confirmation of her lover's feelings in his letters; while she is doubtful about Alfred's commitment, these letters at least are something with which, in a confusing and uncertain situation, she can deal objectively.

During the period when Alfred is away with the army, Fanni depends on his letters not only to reassure her of his love, but also to fill the void created by his departure. The terms which she uses to describe her reception of a letter indicate the extent to which she seeks sustenance in it:

> Quand je reçois une lettre de vous, je l'ouvre avec cet extrême plaisir que je sens en vous voyant. Elle remplit mon désir le plus cher, elle satisfait le besoin le plus pressant de mon cœur. Je la lis avec avidité, elle me plaît, elle m'enchante; et puis après, je l'examine, je pèse chaque mot, je me répète chaque expression, je réfléchis,

je quitte la lettre; je la reprends; elle est les délices de
mes yeux et la joie de mon âme. (LXXIV)

She still devours his letters with the same enthusiasm as before, but now it is to a different end. Because of the enormous significance which she attaches not simply to what he writes, but to the very fact of his writing, her joy at receiving a letter knows no bounds; it is an event which is central to her existence, comparable to nothing else: "Jamais la veille d'un bal paré une coquette ne reçut un écrin rempli de pierreries avec autant de plaisir que j'ai ressenti en voyant ces trois feuilles écrites partout" (LXXXIV).

Letters have such a capital importance for Fanni that in some respects the paper seems to replace its writer. The eventual result of dealing with the letter rather than with the lover is the personification of the former; letters gain an existence of their own, independent of their creator. Fanni dissociates Alfred's letters from Alfred himself to the point of viewing the two as rivals for her attention: "Que votre lettre est tendre! qu'elle est vive! qu'elle est jolie! je l'aime... Je l'aime mieux que vous; je vous quitte pour la relire" (XII). Tangible proof of Alfred's devotion, it is more dependable than Alfred himself and, therefore, easier to love: even over the course of several readings, it will not change. Fanni, who is prone to lavish her affections on the letters she receives, is by the same token playfully jealous of the attention conferred on those which she writes: "*Cette lettre est vue d'abord; elle est baisée, tendrement baisée...* Heureuse lettre! et moi je n'ai rien" (LX).

If the letter may be the source of greatest joy, it may also be a source of disappointment when it does not fulfill expectations. In that case, it is easier to condemn the missive than the lover himself, just as at other times one may prefer to adore it in his stead. Displeased with what Alfred has written her, Fanni execrates the letter as though it *were* Alfred: "Je l'ai lue cent fois, toujours avec humeur, en la rejetant, en lui faisant une mine horrible. Enfin je l'avais bannie de ma présence; un arrêt de la chambre-haute la reléguait tout au fond du tiroir: je viens de la rappeller" (LXXIX). Letters take on various attributes according to whether their contents are welcome or unwelcome; thus the letter of which she speaks in the preceding passage is qualified at another moment as "cold" and "studied." [13]

Letters have a life of their own and for this reason, in the absence of the loved one, they are the best substitute. Fanni insists on the superiority of the letter to the portrait, which cannot move the beholder nearly so much as does the written word: "Le voilà, ce portrait: qu'il est différent de vous. Votre lettre vous rend bien mieux, elle me parle au moins, et le sentiment plus habile que l'artiste, m'offre ces traits chéris que je cherche vainement dans cette image" (XLIII). Fanni's spirited disregard for propriety appears again in the criticism she makes of the portrait in letter XLVI: "Je vais me mettre au lit, votre portrait y vient avec moi, nous allons dormir ensemble... dormir! Ce portrait-là ne vous ressemble guère, il ne vous ressemble point du tout." Letters, by contrast, are less fixed, less immobile than portraits; they vibrate with an inner life which endears them to the recipient. [14] Because a letter is more than a simple representation of the writer, and actually participates in his life, it has the faculty of reducing distance to naught by bringing a part of the loved one to his mistress.

In the long and florid eulogy of the epistolary art which appears in letter LXXVIII, Fanni explains that letters constitute a double bond because, while giving pleasure to the reader, they also provide satisfaction for the writer. One is, she maintains, not only delighted to receive them, but "enchanted" to write them as well. And for Fanni Butlerd, indeed, writing is a veritable mania: she may even compose three letters to Alfred in the space of a single day — at 7 p.m., midnight, and 3 a.m. (LXXXVII-LXXXIX). The letters which she writes are, in fact, an even

---

[13] This tendency to direct emotions at letters rather than at their writers also appears in Juliette Catesby, who says of the letter informing her of her fiancé's infidelity, "Cette lettre... cette odieuse, inexplicable lettre" (XVIII).

[14] Fanni is not the only sensitive soul to remark on the fact that letters seem to live and breathe and speak as no portrait can; Danceny in *Les Liaisons dangereuses* makes a similar observation: "Mais une lettre est le portrait de l'âme. Elle n'a pas, comme une froide image, cette stagnance si éloignée de l'amour; elle se prête à tous nos mouvements: tour à tour elle s'anime, elle jouit, elle se repose" (Choderlos de Laclos, *Les Liaisons dangereuses*, ed. Yves Le Hir [Paris: Garnier, 1961], p. 351).

greater source of consolation to her than those which she receives, for writing is an important security device and a mainstay — all the more so when the lover is either absent or fickle. The great virtue of writing is that a problematic addressee may in a sense be suppressed and the more or less imagined second person of the letter allowed to replace him. If the loved one is gone, or if his affections are unsure, the woman can still deal with something apart from herself — the paper. This is the motif of many of the letters which Fanni writes after becoming Alfred's mistress; the letter allows her to objectify confused and uncertain thoughts by putting them on paper.

Throughout *Lettres de Fanni Butlerd,* writing has a therapeutic value; as Fanni says in letter XL, "J'écris pour écrire." Her mentality in this regard is the same as that of the heroines of the novels upon which this one is modeled. The Portuguese nun, nearly a century earlier, said the same thing; realizing that her letters may not be read by the addressee, she goes on writing nonetheless, observing to the absent "other": "J'écris plus pour moi que pour vous." [15] The heroine of Mme de Graffigny, that other famous writer of love letters to a faithless and distant lover, is in the same tradition: since Aza's whereabouts is a mystery, Zilia knows that her letters have little chance of being delivered to him but she continues to write in order to soothe her troubled soul. Such is the case in *Lettres de Fanni Butlerd,* where the heroine is no more deterred from writing than is Zilia by the possibility that her letters will not be delivered: "Je commence ma lettre sans savoir si vous l'aurez: celle de demain m'annoncera peut-être votre retour. N'importe, j'écris toujours, c'est un plaisir pour moi de vous parler" (LXXXVII). She writes at least as much to satisfy her own needs as to communicate with Alfred.

For all these heroines, writing is at times a sort of happy delusion, an effort to rectify what is imperfect or disquieting in their situations. This is why Zilia is panic-stricken when her "quipos" run out (she is supposedly composing her letters in the Incan manner, by tying knots in colored cords) and she can no longer

---

[15] Guilleragues, *Lettres portugaises,* ed. F. Deloffre and J. Rougeot (Paris: Garnier, 1962), p. 58.

register her thoughts, not yet knowing the French language: "L'illusion me quitte, l'affreuse vérité prend sa place, mes pensées errantes, égarées dans le vuide immense de l'absence, s'anéantiront désormais avec la même rapidité que le tems. Cher Aza, il me semble que l'on nous sépare encore une fois, que l'on m'arrache de nouveau à ton amour." [16] Similarly, Fanni exclaims, "Je sens toujours du regret en finissant une lettre. Cesser de t'écrire, c'est te quitter" (LXXVI). Years earlier, the Portuguese nun had made a like observation: "il me semble que je vous parle, quand je vous écris, et que vous m'êtes un peu plus présent." [17] Writing is a way of pretending that an absence is really a presence.

In spite of Fanni's dependence on letters, she is lucid enough to be aware of the shortcomings of an affair by correspondence. Writing is not speaking and therefore involves certain peculiar difficulties — for example, in the question of arguments. In proportion to the writer's enthusism for the pen is the likelihood that disputes may become interminable. In person one can kiss and make up, but commerce by letter means that one may write for pages and pages, often only worsening matters:

> De près on peut se brouiller; un baiser interrompt la dispute, et fait oublier au milieu de l'explication le sujet de la querelle; mais de loin, eh, bon Dieu, on ne finit pas. *Vous m'avez dit, vous ne deviez pas me dire, je ne croyais pas, il fallait penser, je ne méritais pas, je suis piqué, touché, fâché.* (LXXIV) [18]

This is the inevitable result of the seriousness with which one tends to view the written word; a written affront, continually present before the reader's eyes, is not easily forgotten.

If writing is essential to the woman who is in love, the case is different for the man who, like Alfred, loves less well. A leitmotif in *Lettres de Fanni Butlerd,* as in Crébillon's *Lettres*

---

[16] Mme de Graffigny, *Lettres d'une Péruvienne,* ed. Gianni Nicoletti (Bari, Italy: Adriatica Editrice, 1967), p. 219.

[17] *Lettres portugaises,* p. 58.

[18] Cf. Valmont, in a letter to Mme de Tourvel: "on écrit des volumes, et l'on explique mal ce qu'un quart d'heure suffit pour faire bien entendre" (*Les Liaisons dangereuses,* p. 86).

de la marquise, is the woman's complaints that her lover is an unreliable or sporadic correspondent. Alfred, whose ardor wanes after he has seduced Fanni, writes fewer and shorter letters as time goes on. The Marquise de M***, noticing the same tendency in her lukewarm lover, observes that there is a direct relationship between the passion one feels and the amount one writes: "Mes lettres sont ennuyeuses, et je doute que vous ayez assez de patience pour les achever. Si, comme vous, j'aimais faiblement, elles seraient plus courtes que les vôtres que je les trouverais encore trop longues." [19] That men are less fervid and less dependable correspondents than women was noted by one real-life heroine as well: Julie de Lespinasse, in her correspondence with M. de Guibert, continually laments the infrequency of his letters. He is simply unable to understand, she says, what it means to her to receive a letter from the man she loves; like the Marquise de M***, Julie attributes this to the fact that he loves only imperfectly. (Guibert, with more insight than generosity, compared his unhappy mistress to Fanni Butlerd who, he told her, had similar complaints. Needless to say, Julie resented the comparison, declaring herself "blessée de ce rapprochement que vous faisiez de mon malheur à cette situation de roman.") [20] These women know that an unenthusiastic lover takes no more pleasure in reading letters than he does in composing them. Fanni, like the Marquise who doubts that the Count has sufficient patience to finish her letters, worries constantly about boring Alfred. His letters seem only too short to her, and she rejoices each time she discovers two pages in an envelope instead of one; on the other hand, she frequently apologizes for her own letters: "Je soupe demain chez ma sœur, je bâille d'avance: j'ai bien peur que ma lettre ne vous en fasse faire autant" (LXXXII).

Just as the beginning of Fanni's love affair coincides with a newfound dependence on her correspondence, the end of it is heralded by her refusal to continue writing. The decision to

---

[19] Crébillon fils, *Lettres de la marquise de M*** au comte de R**** (Paris: Le Divan, 1930), p. 119. Mme Riccoboni strikes a similar note in her letters to Liston, e. g. "Si j'écoutais mon cœur, j'aurais beaucoup à dire, mais je serais trop monotone et j'ennuyerais mon cher Bob" (N. 69).
[20] *Lettres,* p. 251.

terminate the letters, however, costs the heroine no end of effort: it is as difficult to renounce her correspondence as it is to give Alfred up. She learns of his intended marriage to another woman just before writing letter CII; it would seem natural that she stop writing immediately, but instead she composes fourteen additional letters. She manifests the same uncertainty as she did when she first fell in love with Alfred and he was so importunate; once again, she engages by letter in reasoning and argumentation. Initially hurt and angered by the revelation of his duplicity, Fanni writes several letters to protest his betrayal; determined not to see him again, she perceives no contradiction in announcing this resolve in a fairly long letter. Alfred meanwhile insists that he is entering into a *mariage de convenance* and that he will continue to love only her. In the face of these assurances she temporarily relents and writes one more love letter in the old style: "C'est donc à mon amant, à mon cher amant, que j'écris? Il m'aime, il m'a toujours aimée; il le dit, il le jure, et je le crois: eh, pourquoi voudrais-je douter de son cœur, moi qui ne vis, ne respire qu'autant que je crois lui être chère?" (CX). It is not long, however, before she begins to shrink back before the impossibility of the situation and the wrong she is doing not only to herself, but to Alfred's future wife: "Quel droit ai-je de causer à une autre les peines que je sens? Pourquoi voudrais-je désoler une femme qui ne m'a point offensée?" (CXIII).[21] She finalizes the rupture by demanding the return of all her letters.

Breaking off is thus a very slow procedure; if it were a question of accomplishing this in person rather than by letter, the business would probably be expedited more quickly. But Fanni cannot stop writing. She who remarked at the end of letter XLVI, "Que j'ai de peine à fermer ma lettre,"[22] has, like so many

---

[21] Crébillon's Marquise had advanced the same reason for not wishing to go on seeing her lover after his betrothal to someone else: "Ne vous présentez plus à mes yeux. Je sais trop ce qu'il en coûte d'aimer sans être aimée, pour contribuer à donner ce chagrin à Mademoiselle de la S***" (*Lettres de la marquise*, pp. 200-01).

[22] Cf. the Portuguese nun, who says "j'ai plus de peine à finir ma lettre que vous n'en avez eu à me quitter, peut-être, pour toujours" (*Lettres portugaises*, p. 58). The last of Mme Riccoboni's extant letters to Liston, dated September 18, 1783, ends in a similarly poignant manner: "Adieu. J'ai peine à vous quitter. C'est une folie, n'est-ce pas?" (N. 141).

epistolary heroines, a sort of *manie écrivante;* from the obsession of writing she can extricate herself only with the utmost difficulty, and so she allows the moribund relationship to drag on. She ultimately makes what appears to be the final break in letter CXIV, and more than a month passes without any exchange. Fanni resumes writing in order to repeat, in letter CXV, her demand that Alfred return her letters; but even after receiving them, she is still unable to leave her pen at rest, so she addresses a last rebuff to her erstwhile lover, reinforced by her decision to publish the letters:

> Je vous dois une réponse, Milord, et je veux vous la faire; mais comme j'ai renoncé à vous, à votre amour, à votre amitié, à la plus légère marque de votre souvenir, c'est dans les papiers publics que je vous l'adresse. Vous me reconnaîtrez: un style qui vous fut si familier, qui flatta tant de fois votre vanité, n'est point encore étranger pour vous. (CXVI)

This letter runs on for several pages; Fanni berates Alfred for the pain he caused her, accuses him of calculatedly lying and deceiving, compares him to men everywhere — "monstres féroces," all of them. She denies him the right even to her friendship, but the most severe and symbolic punishment, to her mind, is that he may never again behold her handwriting: "vos yeux ne reverront jamais ces caractères que vous nommiez *sacrés,* que vous baisiez avec tant d'ardeur, qui vous étaient si *chers* et que vous m'avez fait remettre avec tant d'exactitude." All her letters having at last been returned, she vows to write no more.

When Fanni observes to Alfred in this letter that he will recognize her style even if she does not sign her name, she has good reason to think that this will be the case. The style of *Lettres de Fanni Butlerd* is distinctive and goes a long way toward explaining the novel's continuing appeal. Fanni's writing, lively, spontaneous and immensely varied, has a character which may perhaps best be described as theatrical. For one thing, she frequently affects the present tense to describe either past or future actions, for example when she imagines Alfred's next visit to her: "Il vient, me disais-je, il entre, il va m'embrasser; je connais ce pas vif et léger, j'entends cette voix dont le ton si doux, si caressant, éveille le plaisir dans mon cœur" (XLVIII);

for another, she uses onomatopoeias like "pan," "crac," or "pouf." In these ways, Fanni creates scenes which are both visual and auditive, in spite of the vagueness of the setting and the general absence of detail. Fanni has, moreover, a gift for painting tableaux which resemble stage settings: "C'est pour le coup que Miss Betzi pouvait dire que j'avais l'air d'une Princesse de roman. Votre portrait sur ma table, vos lettres éparses dans mon sein, sur mes genoux, le tiroir renversé, le portefeuille ouvert, je contemplais *mes richesses*" (LXXVIII). It is as though the curtain rises on the heroine's room; its very disorder speaks of her emotional state.

At other moments, Fanni speaks of herself and Alfred in the third person, as though she were a spectator watching them perform. This happens especially when she has offended Alfred; by asking pardon for the faults of an undetermined person, whom she refers to only as "elle," she spares herself the humiliation of having to apologize for herself:

> Elle a chagriné celui qu'elle aime: au lieu du plaisir qu'elle pouvait lui donner, qu'il attendait, qu'il méritait, elle lui a causé de la peine; il a grondé, boudé, chiffonné la Lettre qu'il aurait baisée; il l'a jetée, reprise, mordue, déchirée, il en a mangé la moitié; il est fâché, bien fâché; ah, voilà de belles affaires!... Il faut demander pardon.... Allons, *la méchante* se rend justice, elle est devant vous les yeux baissés, l'air triste... Je vois couler ses larmes, elle plie un genou, vite, mon cher Alfred, relevez-la; qu'un doux souris lui prouve que vous êtes capable d'oublier ses fautes. (XXIII)

Fanni's humor and piquant charm are at their best in this brisk and rhythmical passage, where she describes what she imagines her lover's reaction to her letter must have been and how she would beg pardon if she were with him — as though the writer were really observing both these scenes being played out before her eyes. At the passage's end, she assumes the role of stage director, indicating not only the gestures and bearing of "la méchante," but also the manner in which Alfred's forgiveness should be manifested. The same verve leads Fanni to set up imaginary dialogues between herself and Alfred: like Marivaux's Marianne, she imitates spoken style when she declares that she could never seriously consider the proposal that Alfred has made her: "fixer un moment? prendre un jour?... Oh, cela m'est impossible! Je ne puis vous donner ma parole; n'exigez pas que je vous la donne, je ne le pourrai jamais, je vous en prie, ne l'exigez pas. Je ne saurais. Taisez-vous donc... Oh, tais-toi" (XXX). The terms in which she refuses, of course, reveal her fundamental attitude: she is sorely tempted and her consent will not be long in coming.

One of the main ingredients of Fanni's style is the suspended utterance. While, as indicated earlier, characters in letter-novels (including most of the subsequent novels of Mme Riccoboni) frequently resort to this device in order to communicate the strain under which they are laboring, in *Lettres de Fanni Butlerd* it is put to a more interesting use: through it she suggests the conclusion to a thought which she does not *want* to articulate clearly. Speaking of what her reaction would be if Alfred's letter, which has been delayed in transit, were already in her possession, she uses the suspension to hint broadly at the possibility of indiscretion or impropriety on her part: "Je la lirais vite, vite, et puis doucement, doucement; je la lirais encore, et puis je la... mais je ne veux pas tout dire" (XIV). She concludes letter XXI with the same device: "Ah, que je vous aime! Je vous aime tant, que si vous étiez là... Je vous aimerais trop."

Not only is Fanni's style one of the keys to the novel's success, but there is added richness in the fact that she herself frequently reflects on the character of her writing and of her lover's. The question of style is, for Fanni, fraught with significance; her own, she repeats, is the direct result of the way she feels, and she prides herself on its naturalness. Fanni claims that, always without pretense, she writes on the spur of the moment and records with sincerity and abandon the sentiments to which she is prey: "mon style est toujours assujetti aux impressions que mon âme reçoit. Je ne saurais prendre un ton que je serais forcée d'étudier" (LXV). This is what accounts for the variety of styles which show up in her letters: "J'écris vite, je ne saurais rêver à ce que je veux dire; ma plume court, elle suit ma fantaisie: mon style est tendre quelquefois, tantôt badin, tantôt grave, triste même, souvent ennuyeux, toujours vrai" (LXXVIII). The possibility of such variety is surely one of the virtues of the letter form. Style, as a reflection of sentiment, is molded anew by each successive nuance of feeling which the letter-writer experiences; the letter does not simply describe the happiness of unhappiness of its writer, it is the consequence and expression of those states. The more sensitive the writer, then, the more varied should be his mannèr. Uniformity is tantamount either to coldness or to artifice. [23]

Alfred, according to Fanni, presents his thoughts in a more orderly fashion than does she; early in the novel, she marvels at his capacity for organization: "Vous dites si bien, si précisément ce que vous voulez dire ... Avez-vous plus d'esprit que moi?" (IX). As the affair progresses, it becomes clear that he is not more clever but more calculating, that his expression is exact only because he lacks her warmth and sincerity. Of one of his letters, she complains, "elle me semblait écrite, parce qu'il fallait écrire; les termes étaient ceux qui expriment la passion, mais la tournure me paraissait froide, étudiée" (LXXIX). [24] The real reader, of course, never sees Alfred's letters in full, but Fanni sometimes quotes from them, illustrating the differences in the two styles and in the two writers. "*Je ne vous connais point assez?* Qui vous l'a dit? *Je ne douterais jamais un instant de la sincérité, de l'ardeur, de la vérité...* Oh, va te promener avec tes plaintes" (LXVII). Here the spontaneity of Fanni's style is used to offset the stilted and meaningless eloquence of Alfred's. Her naturalness is such that, while she continues for a time to write to Alfred after her discovery of his infidelity, she nonetheless protests that she can no longer do so with ease: "il m'est difficile, tout à fait difficile, de vous écrire. Le style dont je me servais avec vous n'était pas dans ma plume; le vôtre est encore le même" (CVI). That his style has not changed when the situation has been so radically transformed is the proof that his letters were no more than an exercise in writing.

* * *

---

[23] Valmont in *Les Liaisons dangereuses* goes a logical step further, realizing that disarray is a conventional sign of passion: "j'ai mis beaucoup de soin à ma lettre, et j'ai tâché d'y mettre ce désordre, qui peut seul peindre le sentiment" (p. 141).

[24] Mme Riccoboni herself complained to Robert Liston that one of his letters was "écrite sans passion, et même avec tout le sang-froid national" (N. 76).

When Fanni resolves to write no more, she nevertheless decides to allow herself, if not the pleasure of composing letters, at least the vicarious one of reviewing and immortalizing her previous ones: she determines to publish the correspondence, while concealing her own identity as well as Alfred's. In a short preface to *Lettres de Fanni Butlerd* ("Mistriss Fanni à un seul lecteur"), the novel's reader first learns that it is Fanni herself who is responsible for the publication. Here she begs a "seul lecteur" — obviously Alfred himself — to keep the secret of its authorship, should the collection ever fall into his hands. Here, too, she explains her reasons for publishing:

> Le désir de faire admirer son esprit ne l'engage point à publier ces lettres, mais celui d'immortaliser, s'il est possible, une passion qui fit son bonheur, dont les premières douceurs sont encore présentes à son idée, et dont le souvenir lui sera toujours cher. Non, ce n'est point cette passion qui fit couler ses pleurs, qui porta la douleur et l'amertume dans son âme. Elle n'accuse que vous des maux qu'elle a soufferts; elle ne connaît que vous pour l'auteur de ses peines. Son amour était en elle la source de tous les biens; vous l'empoisonnâtes cruellement! Elle ne hait point l'amour, elle ne hait que vous.

The decision to publish, and in so doing to make the style of her writing a subject for public scrutiny, constitutes a significant break with her past: she succeeds thereby in dispossessing Alfred of the letters, sentiments and manner once intended for him alone, and in refusing him the continued status of lover, but rather transforming him into a kind of public property. There seems to be a ritual for exorcism involved as Fanni, by putting the correspondence as well as the affair itself on a new and impersonal level, attempts to rid herself of Alfred and all that his betrayal represented — in the same way, perhaps, as Mme Riccoboni tried to exorcise an unhappy love affair of her own by publishing a novel based upon it.

Having discovered as early as 1757, with *Lettres de Fanni Butlerd*, the formula for a superior letter-novel — simplicity of plot and unity of form and content — Mme Riccoboni never returned to it. Perhaps, in filling certain of her later works with secondary characters and all manner of accident, she was responding to the influence of the conventional novels of adventure and romance. But it is possible that, after *Lettres de Fanni Butlerd*, Mme Riccoboni lost the largely autobiographical inspiration to build a work entirely around a single character and to create a novel whose interest is almost wholly psychological. More than any of the later works, it seems a veritable *cri du cœur*, the kind of novel an author does not write twice.

CHAPTER IV

VARIATIONS ON A FORMULA

> Il est des moments où l'on aimerait tant à pleurer ensemble.
>
> *Lettres de Sophie de Vallière*

While letter-novels in which the silent addressee is not a central character, and where the letters are therefore concerned primarily with conveying information, are less interesting from a technical standpoint than the *Fanni Butlerd* variety, the advantages of the letter form even there are far from negligible. In the first place, the presence of the letter confers a special reality on its writer because, as Ian Watt points out,

> letters are the most direct material evidence for the inner life of their writers which exist.... Their reality is one which reveals the subjective and private orientations of the writer both towards the recipient and the people discussed, as well as the writer's own inner being.[1]

They provide an effective and immediate expression of that inner being because they are composed at the very moment when the writer is in distress, and in this respect the form differs substantially from memoirs. Neither time nor the consciousness of a third party comes between hero and reader. The sympathies of the real reader are more directly engaged because, in a sense, he replaces the fictional reader in his privileged position as the

---

[1] *The Rise of the Novel: Studies in Defoe, Richardson and Fielding* (Berkeley, 1957), p. 191.

confidant to whom the narrator speaks. In these novels there is an atmosphere of intimacy which does not obtain in the simple first person form: the writer is addressing a friend and therefore describing circumstances in a manner which is different from what he would use if he were writing for an unidentified public. "Ce que je vais vous conter," writes Juliette Catesby, "n'est intéressant que pour un ami" (XIV). This personal character of the letter-novel, lending it appropriately to expression of all the nuances of feeling, must have accounted in a large measure for its enormous popularity.

To such a degree was Mme Riccoboni aware of the many possibilities of the letter, and so cleverly did she manipulate the form and vary the circumstances, that each of her letter-novels has a character which is unique — even those written within the framework of letters by a single writer. The nature, length, quantity and motivation of letters in any given work distinguish it from the others and determine to a large extent the kind of work it is. In this chapter we will take up, in the order of their appearance, the four basically linear letter-novels which followed *Lettres de Fanni Butlerd,* and then consider the last novel which Mme Riccoboni wrote and the only one in which there is more than one active correspondent, *Lettres de Mylord Rivers.*

Lettres de Mylady Juliette Catesby à Mylady Henriette Campley, son amie, which appeared in 1759,[2] is closely related in form to the journal; in this respect it resembles Richardson's first letter-novel, *Pamela,* which becomes a journal as it progresses. The Riccoboni novel is much shorter, however, and the plot is considerably more limited. While Pamela's letters chiefly describe the many and often surprising events in the household of Mr. B., during most of *Lettres de Juliette Catesby* essentially nothing transpires. But like Pamela's letters to her parents,

---

[2] Fréron reviewed the novel in *L'Année littéraire* as early as December 1758 (VIII, 289-302), but I have never seen an edition bearing a 1758 imprint and doubt there was one. The *Correspondance littéraire,* moreover, which appeared twice a month, announced in April 1759 (IV, 98) that *Juliette Catesby* "vient de paraître."

Juliette's are motivated by her sojourn away from home; they are addressed to the confidante whom she has left behind.

Juliette's departure from London is occasioned by the fact that Mylord d'Ossery, the fiancé who inexplicably deserted her two years earler in order to marry another woman, is now widowed and once more pursuing Juliette. Like all sensitive souls, Juliette can choose to reject a lover who has proved himself unworthy, but she cannot prevent herself from continuing to love him; she can escape the man himself, but not the memory of her love: "Le souvenir marche avec nous; on croit le perdre en cherchant le monde, mais un instant de solitude lui rend toute la force que la dissipation semblait lui avoir ôtée" (VI). Juliette attempts to put Ossery out of her mind to the extent that it is possible and devotes her energies largely to keeping a kind of diary of her journey for the benefit of Henriette, her confidante. Her letters often contain mordant descriptions of the places and persons she visits; she tells Henriette, for example, that she has visited the estate of one of the latter's former suitors:

> Miss Bidulf qui, à votre refus, s'est accomodée du cœur, de la main et de toute l'immense personne de Sir George notre hôte, est bien plus propre que vous à lui procurer l'espèce de bonheur qu'il est capable de goûter. (IV)

Her penchant for designing lively and amusing portraits of her hosts and companions lends the novel much color but, like *Lettres de Fanni Butlerd,* this work provides little information about the background of the central figure.

Only after five weeks have elapsed — which is near the end of the novel — does Ossery get the opportunity to explain his behavior to Juliette; at this juncture, she ends her vignettes and character portrayals and applies herself to settling with him. The reconciliation is achieved as the result of a letter which he sends to Juliette, the only moment in the novel when a letter becomes a factor in the plot. Ossery resorts to writing to his erstwhile mistress because of her determination to avoid his company; this he explains in a preliminary note:

> L'horreur que vous a fait ma présence, l'état où je vous ai vue, et la douleur que j'ai sentie d'en être la cause,

m'ont déterminé à renoncer au projet de m'approcher de vous sans votre ordre positif. Je consens à vous écrire ce que je voulais vous dire, si vous aviez pu m'écouter. (XXXV)

His suspicion that, although Juliette will not permit him to address her in person, she will consent to read his missive, is well founded: like Mme de Tourvel and like so many other epistolary heroines, Juliette Catesby is easily persuaded to read things to which she would refuse to listen. But in her case it is all to the good, since the letter proves Ossery less unworthy than he originally appeared to be and thereby reunites them.

Since this letter is offered to the public not as emanating directly from Ossery but as Juliette transcribes it for Henriette, care is taken to explain how something as personal as this may be copied and forwarded. The explanation is based on the convention that every young lady has a confidante to whom she tells all. Ossery therefore notes, prefatory to entering into the details of his story: "comme vous pourriez sentir quelque peine en cachant à lady Henriette des faits où vous êtes intéressée, je n'exige pas que vous vous gêniez sur ce point" (XXXV). It is, of course, necessary that the heroine feel free to relay Ossery's story to her confidante; otherwise, the real reader could never know it. But Ossery's suggestion that she do so seems somehow factitious; it damages the impression of authenticity by reminding the reader that Juliette is obliged to copy the story if he is to see it. It might have been preferable simply to let the heroine send the copy and not call attention to any possible breach of confidence involved: protagonists of epistolary novels were not, after all, accustomed to troubling themselves on that score.

What Ossery relates is that a passing infidelity during an evening of revelry resulted in Jenny Monfort's pregnancy; he did the honorable thing and married her, and only now that he is widowed can he reveal to Juliette the reasons for his apparent desertion. This is a familiar novelistic device: seemingly incomprehensible or inexcusable behavior appears justifiable in the light of later discoveries.[3] Since the focus of an individual letter-

---

[3] Perhaps the prototype for such a situation occurs in "Histoire de Monsieur Des Frans et de Sylvie" in *Les Illustres Françaises* of Robert

writer is necessarily narrow, the truth is attainable only when successive accounts of the same event throw new light on the matter. Ossery's letter tells us essentially what we already know from Juliette, but includes details and circumstances which she could not know and which are essential in rehabilitating him: she learns that he was not totally without honor and, however culpable his behavior, his heart always belonged to Juliette. This "game of mirrors," as Versini calls it, was frequently used even before *Les Liaisons dangereuses*: Clarissa Harlowe and Lovelace often recount the same incidents, but while she writes from the point of view and with the limited knowledge of the victim, Lovelace speaks as the seducer whose machinations are at work.

Included within Ossery's story is a letter from Jenny Monfort telling him that she is pregnant. Since Ossery's story is itself incorporated in a letter from Juliette to Henriette, Jenny's letter is twice removed from its original state: the reader sees it only as copied by Juliette from a copy made by Ossery. The inclusion of a letter in an *histoire* which is itself included in a letter was not an uncommon practice, and Mme Riccoboni was to resort more and more to such devices in her later and more complicated works.

While the thirty-seven letters of Juliette Catesby cover a scant six weeks and recount but one episode in her life, Mme Riccoboni's subsequent letter-novel — *Histoire de Miss Jenny, écrite et envoyée par elle à Mylady, Comtesse de Roscomonde, Ambassadrice d'Angleterre à la Cour de Dannemarck* (1764) — tells the story of the heroine's entire life up to the time of writing and, in fact, takes the reader as far back as the birth of Jenny's mother. Moreover, whereas Juliette composes her brief and chatty notes in an effort to distract and console herself, Jenny takes up her pen for a different reason altogether and under more somber circumstances; she seeks approbation more than consolation and — as is evident from the work's title — composes not a journal but a memoir. *Histoire de Miss Jenny* belongs, like *La Vie de Marianne*, to the tradition of memoir-novels written in letter form. Jenny writes, as does Marianne, at the request of a lady friend

---

Challes (1713) where the heroine is objectively guilty of an infidelity for which she is later exonerated.

who is eager to know the details of her life. Customarily in such novels, the hero or heroine claims to be writing for his own amusement and for the sake of having a private record of events, or declares the memoir the result of friendly pressure to reveal the facts of his life; the latter variation means that the novel may be composed in the form of a letter or letters. While Marivaux's heroine sends her story in eleven installments, Jenny writes only two: the first, quite long, constitutes the body of the novel; it is followed by a short note written after a time has elapsed since the conclusion of the memoir. This technique, of course, gives the novel a totally different flavor from *Lettres de Juliette Catesby*: whereas the earlier heroine writes a day-by-day record of events in short, terse notes, Jenny — like Diderot's Sœur Suzanne in *La Religieuse* — tells her story nonstop.

Although Jenny resembles Marianne in that she knows the outcome of the story when she begins it, she differs radically in that she has none of the distance or wisdom of years which are Marianne's when she writes. When Marianne starts her account, she has already found her place in the world as Madame la Comtesse de ***; the events she relates belong to a not too recent past: "Il y a quinze ans que je ne savais pas encore si le sang d'où je sortais était noble ou non, si j'étais bâtarde ou légitime."[4] These uncertainties have presumably long since been resolved and the elder Marianne tells her story with calm and security. Jenny, on the other hand, is still very young when she writes and, like Sœur Suzanne, is temporally much closer to the occurrences which she describes, bringing to them all the emotion with which one composes a letter at the very moment of stress. In fact, she terminates her story saying, "je vous écrirai bientôt du lieu de ma retraite, si pourtant je survis à l'extrême douleur dont je me sens oppressée."

Jenny writes moreover during the heat of controversy regarding the acceptability of her conduct; she takes a backward glance at her life in order to defend herself against criticism which is being leveled against her. Acutely aware of the avid interest which many observers are taking in her, she sees herself

---

[4] *La Vie de Marianne*, pp. 9-10.

at the center of a great drama, as though on a vast stage where her actions are scrutinized and judged:

> Je me vois obligée, Madame, de justifier ma conduite à vos yeux, ou de vous laisser croire qu'elle est très singulière, peut-être très blamable. Par leurs propositions brillantes, deux personnes attirent sur moi l'attention d'une foule de spectateurs. Chacun me juge au gré de ses propres idées, et me comdamne sur ses propres principes. (Part I, p. 11)

Many memorialists offer similar explanations for putting their stories down in writing; for instance, *Histoire de Madame de Montbrillant* by Mme d'Épinay is composed, according to the heroine, in order to justify her behavior and thereby clear her name:

> Je me dois, et je dois à ceux qui m'honorent encore de leur estime et de leur tendresse, de leur laisser les moyens de détruire après moi la calomnie par le récit le plus sincère des différents événements dans lesquels j'ai eu presque toujours les apparences contre moi.[5]

Mme Riccoboni herself uses this fictional pretext even in *Lettres de Madame de Sancerre*, which is not a memoir-novel, at the point where the heroine decides to send her life's story to her confidant: she does so, she explains, because she feels constrained to demonstrate the rationality and intrinsic necessity of her seemingly bizarre behavior. This device alerts the reader that he is about to hear a story both personal and controversial and that he will have to sit in judgment on the protagonist; the real reader becomes, like the fictional reader, not only confidant but also judge.[6]

Jenny is able to excite the reader's interest in a way the strict letter-writer cannot: she knows how pathetically things will turn

---

[5] *Histoire de Madame de Montbrillant*, ed. Georges Roth (Paris: Gallimard, 1951), I, 6. Probably composed in the 1750's and 60's, this work was not published until the nineteenth century (see Roth's introduction).

[6] Cf. Prévost's *Histoire d'une Grecque moderne* (1740), where the reader is directly addressed on several occasions and called on to pass judgment on the character and conduct of the heroine.

out. Although the mystery about the occurrences which she describes has been cleared up in her own mind, she keeps the reader in a state of uncertainty throughout, and he cannot fit all the pieces together until the very end. He always suspects the worst, however, because Jenny (like so many memorialists, notably those of Prévost) repeatedly foreshadows future misfortunes. The rather complex story which eventually emerges is, briefly, the following. The scion of wealthy aristocratic families, Jenny is herself illegitimate and penniless. Fooled by a sham wedding into thinking she has married the ruthless Lord Danby, she eventually discovers the truth and escapes him, only to have Danby kill the man to whom she subsequently becomes engaged. (Jenny's heart all the while belongs to a third man, the Comte de Clare, but she is sacrificing herself out of consideration for her best friend, to whom Clare is betrothed.) After her fiancé's death, she writes her story, sends it to the Comtesse de Roscomonde, and retires from society, probably the most pathetic of the Riccoboni heroines. The novel concludes with a short letter which Jenny, now installed in her retreat, sends to the Countess in order to assure her that she is adjusting to her new and quieter mode of existence.

Mme Riccoboni's next novel displays once more the lightheartedness, the glib remarks and the frivolity which characterize parts of *Lettres de Juliette Catesby*. Published in 1766 and dedicated to David Garrick, *Lettres d'Adélaïde de Dammartin, comtesse de Sancerre, à Monsieur le comte de Nancé, son ami* consists of the letters of a young widow to her friend and confidant while the latter is traveling. This is a novel of manners, which describes a group of aristocratic and idle young women whose principle pastimes are love and gossip. According to Mme Riccoboni herself, "Les mœurs de notre noblesse, c'est-à-dire de notre *noblesse honnête*, le ton de notre cour, facile à outrer, rarement saisi juste, voilà tout le mérite des *Lettres de Madame de Sancerre*" (N. 34). [7] At times the work recalls the description of a witty and elegant

---

[7] She goes on to express her misgivings about the possibility of successfully translating such a novel into English: "Est-ce assez pour se soutenir dans une langue étrangère? Les faits perdent naturellement par la différence des usages, mais les détails tombent absolument par celle du style."

society which we find in the letters of Mme de Sévigné. Unlike the typical Riccoboni heroine who moves in a small circle and has few close friends (sometimes not more than one, the confidant to whom she writes), Mme de Sancerre is integrated into a larger society where she has numerous friends and acquaintances. Her letters, especially the early ones, give brief and colorful portraits of the members of the group, their interests and diversions — which seem to consist chiefly of composing couplets, attending dinner parties until early in the morning, and spending secret weekends in the country.[8]

It is significant that Mme de Sancerre is a widow: this condition is necessary in certain fictional and dramatic situations, because in a society where complete naïveté is assumed prior to marriage, certain roles cannot be filled by unmarried girls. A young unwed woman, for example, could not have a man as her confidant, nor could she occupy the center of a group like the one just described, enjoying perfect freedom to receive both men and women at her leisure and to entertain the suits of a number of admirers. (In Molière's *Misanthrope* Célimène, whose role is similar to that of Mme de Sancerre, is likewise a widow.) The plot revolves around the fact that Mme de Sancerre and her two closest friends, also recently widowed, all find themselves in the throes of a decision about the advisability of remarriage. Because of an unhappy first marriage, Mme de Sancerre has misgivings about falling in love again, but M. de Montalais wins her heart; there is, however, an obstacle to their love: Montalais himself is married. But the wife with whom he is united in a *mariage de convenance* is unattractive and sickly, and has "la manie d'avoir des héritiers."[9]

---

[8] Servais Etienne may well have had this novel in mind when he wrote of Mme Riccoboni, "Elle donne mieux que tous, non l'image, mais l'idée de la bonne compagnie" (*Le Genre romanesque en France* [Paris, 1922], p. 313).

[9] James Foster says of Mme Riccoboni's novels, "Often lovers are kept apart because one of them is married, and there is nothing to do but wait for the undertaker. This is the oft-derided 'Riccoboni situation' and, of course, it does have its dubious aspects" (*History of the Pre-Romantic Novel in England* [New York: MLA, 1949], p. 147). In fact, the situation occurs three times: here, in *Histoire de Miss Jenny* and in *Lettres de Juliette Catesby*.

Mme de Sancerre's integration into a large social group seems to be accompanied by a certain weakness of character: she is a less forceful personality than the other, more solitary, Riccoboni heroines, and unable to take the kind of decisive action which her situation indicates. When she realizes that she is in love with a married man, Mme de Sancerre decides that she must flee; but, unlike Juliette Catesby who also determines to avoid the man she loves, Mme de Sancerre finds it impossible to tear herself away, and for one reason and another keeps postponing her departure. She ends several letters to Nancé with the assurance that she is about to leave, but each time the following communication begins with an explanation of her delay: she eventually starts using the dateline "Toujours Paris." Fortunately for Mme de Sancerre, Montalais' wife dies in childbirth, but at this point there is another complication: an extravagant and long-lost cousin of the heroine threatens her with financial ruin unless she marries him. In the end, however, he relents and she weds Montalais. [10]

This work is distinct among Mme Riccoboni's novels in its relatively large number of important figures. Mme de Sancerre is the central character, but the fate of her two friends, their suitors, her own suitor, his wife, and several other acquaintances is also at issue. The exposition is somewhat difficult to follow because of the realistic presentation of all these plots and subplots: Mme de Sancerre mentions a host of names in her first letter to Nancé — who is presumably acquainted with the people of whom she speaks — and no special effort is made to identify them for the reader, who is able to sort out the various components only gradually as he acquires more information. Contemporary critics, who appreciated the novel more as a love story than as a novel

---

[10] The episode concerning the cousin, one of the most romantic and far-fetched in the novel, was adapted for the stage in 1777 by Boutet de Monvel; the play, called *L'Amant bourru,* was quite successful (see Crosby, pp. 163-64). It follows the novel closely, except that it eliminates Montalais' first wife, so that Mme de Sancerre's love for him becomes more palatable. Oddly, the letter device is used to relate much of the action on stage, even though the episode could surely be better presented through dialogue, since all those who figure in it are in the same vicinity and a confrontation would have dramatic appeal; the letter technique apparently impressed the dramatist as sufficiently closely related to the story line so that he felt obliged to retain some of the letters in the play.

of manners,[11] objected to this confusion. The *Correspondance littéraire*, for example, commented, "Le commencement du roman est un peu embrouillé et embarrassé de détails obscurs dont on ne sent pas encore la nécessité."[12] Nor, for that matter, was it apparently a very great success.

A further distinguishing element in *Lettres de Madame de Sancerre* is that here the confidant is a man. Because confidants in letter-novels were commonly of the same sex as the writers (e.g. Lovelace and Belford; Clarissa and Anna Howe; Julie and Claire; Saint-Preux and Milord Edouard), the title of this novel — in which a man is mentioned as the correspondent of Mme de Sancerre — probably gave many readers the initial idea that the heroine was corresponding with a lover. But the addressee is not the lover (or "antagonist" as François Jost labels him)[13]; Nancé plays the same role as Henriette, the confidante in *Lettres de Juliette Catesby:* he is maintained strictly outside the action and we know almost nothing about him.

Mme Riccoboni's last novel of this type is more complicated than any of the others: *Lettres d'Élisabeth-Sophie de Vallière à Louise-Hortence de Canteleu, son amie* (1771) incorporates elements of both the journal and the memoir and is, in fact, a mystery story. It is an intricate work, divided into two distinct parts, with a structure which Henri Coulet terms "dense et complexe":

> les deux parties du roman sont très différentes, la première est un roman psychologique et sentimental, dans le goût de la première moitié du siècle, la seconde, qui raconte des faits antérieurs, est un roman de couleur sombre, aux caractères étranges et aux événements troublants, bien que l'auteur laisse deviner une explication

---

[11] See, for example, article on *Lettres de Madame de Sancerre* in the *Monthly Review:* "The progress of the tender passion through all the embarrassing situations and circumstances peculiar to a delicate mind, is finely described, and makes the principal subject of these volumes" (XXXVII [July 1767], p. 68).

[12] VII (November 1766), 164-65.

[13] "Ici d'emblée, on soupçonne des lettres à l'antagoniste" (*Europeana*, pp. 124-25).

logique à la force posthume d'une malédiction paternelle; le dénouement les unit très solidement...[14]

The first half of the novel poses the enigma of Sophie's origin and the second half deliberately solves it, the resolution being brought about by a chance encounter between Sophie and Lindsey, the former lover of her long dead mother.

Sophie's father, like that of the heroine of *Histoire de Miss Jenny*, died before she was born, and her mother, again like Jenny's, died very soon afterwards. The two characters therefore resemble each other in their unpropitious beginnings, but in Sophie's case the problem with which she must cope is the uncertainty of her origins, whereas for Jenny the nature of her illegitimate birth is never in doubt; while Sophie's task is to prove that she is of aristocratic stock, Jenny's is to win a place in society in spite of her illegitimacy. The difference in the situations of the two heroines is related to the difference in novel structure: Jenny has only to *present* her background, which she does in the form of a memoir; Sophie has to *discover* hers, and the novel becomes an investigation. It opens with seventeen-year-old Sophie's realization that she is not, as she has always believed, the niece of the noblewoman who raised her; her protectress has just died and when her papers reveal that her charge is a mere foundling, she is turned out by the family and separated from the man she loves, the Marquis de Germeuil. The expression of her love for Germeuil and of her despair at the futility of that love predominates in the letters she sends to her confidante throughout the first half of the novel; the second half is concerned with the long story told by Lindsey — an account which illuminates Sophie's origins and makes it possible for her and Germeuil to marry. His somber and melancholy narration takes the reader through England, America, Holland and France, and tells of Sophie's beautiful and ill-starred mother and the tragic misunderstanding between the two men who loved her. It is replete with drama: a tyrannical father, a deathbed curse, a secret marriage, and a fatal duel followed by a death by heartbreak. But in spite

---

[14] *Le Roman jusqu'à la Révolution* (Paris: Armand Colin, 1967), pp. 385-86.

of these adventurous elements and an extraordinary number of coincidences, the work is artistically viable: the connection between the parts of the drama is never lost from sight and, in the end, the pieces of the puzzle fit snugly into place. The conclusion, moreover, establishes a kind of retroactive justice, with Sophie and Lindsey enabling each other to find the happiness which her parents never knew, and which they themselves had been so long denied.

As the content of these novels becomes more complex, the structure reflects this complexity. Letter length and the other mechanical aspects of technique accommodate themselves to their adventurous nature; *Histoire de Miss Jenny*, *Lettres de Sophie de Vallière* and, to a lesser extent, *Lettres de Madame de Sancerre* have a number of *tiroirs*. This of course was a common device which, among other advantages, allowed an author to accumulate many pages of text without resolving the main plot, but Mme Riccoboni generally makes a close connection between it and the interpolations. In *Lettres de Sophie de Vallière*, for example, Lindsey's story occupies half the novel and takes the reader far back in time, but, as we have seen, it is not gratuitous: the heroine is intimately involved in it and, moreover, the story is punctuated with Sophie's reactions and guesses regarding its implications for her.

Mme Riccoboni's single-writer letter-novels thus range from the very simple to the complex: *Lettres de Fanni Butlerd* is the story of one incident in the life of the heroine, and *Lettres de Juliette Catesby* is only slightly more complicated. It too concerns a single episode in the heroine's life, although there are a few interpolated stories and several backward glances. In these works there are few main characters and most of the major events are interior. After these novels there is a change: the works become longer, the cast of characters is increased and the action becomes more intricate and more dispersed. There is, nonetheless, a certain undeniable sameness about the novels just discussed, especially regarding the figure of the heroine: invariably innocent, she is in some way victimized. But each one has a distinctive personality: the witty and caustic Juliette, the irresolute Mme de Sancerre and the frail Sophie do not readity fit into the same mold. The external trappings of the novels, particularly the geographical and social milieux, differ somewhat as well. Likewise, there is considerable variety of tone. While *Histoire de Miss Jenny* (which, like *Lettres de Fanni Butlerd*, asserts the illusory nature of true happiness for the sensitive woman) is patently pessimistic, *Lettres de Juliette Catesby* and *Lettres de Madame de Sancerre*, in spite of the setbacks and sufferings which the heroines experience, are essentially optimistic in outlook: a good deal of gaiety prevails throughout and both heroines, in the end, marry the men they love. *Lettres de Sophie de Vallière* falls between the two extremes: Sophie does finally marry Germeuil, but she first traverses a string of hardships, she anguishes right up to the end — and even then her sufferings have so conditioned her that she is scarcely able to believe in her good fortune. Finally, within the limits of the particular form, Mme Riccoboni used a number of variations, and created not just love stories, but a mystery, a novel of manners, a memoir-novel and a journal. After *Lettres de Sophie de Vallière*, she would seem to have explored most of the possibilities of the linear formula. The trend, moreover, was toward the letter-novel to which several characters contribute, and towards the end of her career as a writer, she tried her hand at this.

The structure of the last novel, then, *Lettres de Mylord Rivers à Sir Charles Cardigan, entremêlées d'une partie de ses correspondances à Londres pendant son séjour en France* (1776), distinguishes it from all the earlier works. There are four principal correspondents, among whom takes place a real exchange of opinion and information. Not the content of the letters alone, but their number and disposition as well, are significant. Forty-six letters make up the novel — of which thirty are written by Rivers to his various friends, and fifteen are addressed to him by these same friends. The forty-sixth and final letter is written by a friend of Rivers to a hitherto unmentioned party, informing her of the happy ending to Rivers' story.

What is initially striking is that here (as in *Histoire du Marquis de Cressy*, the first of Mme Riccoboni's two non-letter-novels), the central figure is a male. But, unlike the Marquis of the earlier work, Rivers is a romantic hero: young and handsome like Cressy, he is also sensitive, kind and generous. Rivers has none of the unattractive characteristics which Mme Riccoboni so often associates with her male protagonists; he is, on the contrary, a sort of male version of her most attractive heroines. It would seem that a principal letter-writer, according to Mme Riccoboni's system, had to be an admirable figure; the main difference between Rivers and the usual female protagonist is that, while a Juliette Catesby or a Sophie de Vallière devotes her powers of intellect chiefly to analysis of the heart, Rivers also likes to philosophize. The philosophical aspect of this novel places it in the tradition of *Lettres persanes* and *Lettres péruviennes:* the hero is a naive stranger, who travels abroad and confides his observations about the foreign country to friends at home. Rivers is supposedly an Englishman visiting France. Through him, the author criticizes certain trends in contemporary society, especially the attitudes of the philosophes or pseudo-philosophes. For example, Rivers repeatedly censures Sir George, a friend of Charles who, by the "ardent amour pour l'humanité" which he professes, appears to be a caricature of the philosophes. "En pensant trop au bien général," Rivers warns, "crains de négliger le bien particulier ... *Aimer les hommes!* aimer *tous les hommes!* eh mais, c'est n'aimer rien..." (III). [15] His own aspirations, Rivers insists, are modest: he seeks not to alleviate the misery of mankind at large, but simply to practice generosity and compassion toward his friends and family; spurning fame and glory, he desires only the friendship and benevolence of those around him.

In an early letter to Cardigan, Rivers, like Montesquieu's Persian, points out that a foreigner needs time to adjust to a city and to begin to fit in: "Avant de me laisser présenter, je veux m'accoutumer aux inflexions de la langue française, et m'étudier à perdre, s'il est possible, cet air étranger qu'en tous pays on doit plus, je crois, à sa contenance, qu'à sa physionomie" (II). When his friends at home press him for insights into the character of the French nation, Rivers insists that he has little talent for that sort of thing; he will make no judgments on the French, merely

---

[15] These remarks are strikingly reminiscent of those of Damis in Palissot's satire *Les Philosophes* (1760): "Et pour en parler vrai, ma foi, je les soupçonne / D'aimer le genre humain, mais pour n'aimer personne" (Act II, sc. 5).

some superficial observations. The metaphor by which Rivers expresses this idea is theatrical:

> Je suis assez dans le monde comme sont au théâtre ces paisibles spectateurs qui, cherchant à s'amuser de la pièce, l'écoutent sans s'embarrasser si elle pouvait être mieux faite, mieux écrite, et quelquefois maudissent un voisin trop difficile ou trop instruit, plus fâchés de perdre une partie de leur plaisir, que satisfaits d'être éclairés par sa critique. (II)

Rivers' ideas on this subject would seem to be Mme Riccoboni's own, and at moments like this one senses the presence of the actress-author who, even years after leaving the stage and at the end of her literary career, instinctively prefers a public of enthusiasts caught up in the play to a critical and analytical audience.

Its philosophical content notwithstanding, *Lettres de Mylord Rivers* is fundamentally a love story. The object of his trip, as he observes at the very start, is "ni le dessein de comparer deux nations rivales, ni cette mélancolie vague, qui porte une foule de nos compatriotes à passer la mer"; his departure from London is occasioned rather by the realization that he is in love with his pupil Adeline Rutland — who, unbeknownst to Rivers, shares his feelings. The story, as it develops in his correspondence with his friends in London, involves the efforts of a number of people to bring Adeline and Rivers together by convincing them of this reciprocity. The love interest, then, accounts for the hero's temporary expatriation, while its resolution brings about his return and the conclusion of the correspondence.

Fifteen of the thirty letters which Rivers composes in France — a total of one third of the work — are directed to Sir Charles Cardigan, his closest friend. Strangely, though, his answers never appear, while the answers of others of Rivers' correspondents do. But that Charles does respond is certain because Rivers continually refers to what Charles has written; his first letter, for example, begins: "J'ai reçu ta lettre, Charles." This is perhaps a remnant of the one-sided letter technique which Mme Riccoboni had hitherto practiced, where the confidant's responses are not seen, his function being to serve as a depository for the complaints and observations of the main protagonist; he is a listener, not a speaker, and his opinions appear only as they are filtered through the mind of the central figure. It seems that this concept of confidant was too much a part of Mme Riccoboni's fictional apparatus to be abandoned even in a novel with many writers. And so Sir Charles, unlike Belford and unlike Mylord Edouard, enjoys only a vague and vicarious reality.

All but one of the remaining fifteen letters which Rivers writes are sent to ladies: to Cardigan's wife Mary, to his sister Lady Orrery, and to Rivers' protégée Adeline. Their responses constitute the remainder. The correspondence with the three women centers on affairs of the heart: Lady Mary and Lady Orrery speak to Rivers of their love life and try to pry into his. They attempt to inform him obliquely of Adeline's love, while making every effort to extract an avowal of his feelings for her. Because there is no real plot, the "action" consists (and there are of course parallels in Marivaux's theater) in the uniting of two people who already love each other and must be induced to admit it — something which in person they were unable to do.

The central couple exchange only nine letters, five by Rivers and four by Adeline. Far from being love letters, these are concerned almost exclusively with mutual criticism and the expression of hurt and displeasure on both sides. The very fact that there are so few and that they are filled with recriminations is an indication of their difficulty in communicating. The disposition of their letters is equally significant. Well before the appearance of Adeline's first letter to her tutor, he complains to his other friends of her long silence which, he says, troubles and saddens him. Yet he avoids writing directly to her — even though everyone suggests that she is only waiting for him to do just that. It is a long and painful process for either of the two to address a letter to the other, and the first exchange is the fourteenth letter of the novel. Adeline's letter to Rivers is itself indicative of her discomfiture in that it is shorter than the average letter. Her intention in writing, moreover, is to convey her annoyance at Rivers: "Conviendrait-il à la reconnaissante pupille de Mylord Rivers, de s'apercevoir qu'il peut avoir tort?" (XIV). Subsequent letters between them serve more to sharpen antagonism than to effect an understanding. Rivers is so far from perceiving Adeline's real disposition that he suspects her of incapacity for love; he returns to a theatrical metaphor to warn her that the person who never loves only becomes more unhappy as time goes by:

> Le personnage de spectateur peut satisfaire tant que des nouveautés varient la scène. Mais quand on a tout vu, l'uniformité de la représentation lasse les yeux et plus encore l'attention. On cesse de rire des faiblesses de l'humanité; on les remarque avec humeur; les ridicules choquent, les travers irritent, la déraison révolte. Tout déplaît, on devient chagrin, misanthrope; on hait, on est haï, et l'on finit par ne trouver dans ce monde où pour se singulariser on a choisi de vivre à l'écart, que des sujets d'ennui, de dégoût et d'amertume. (XXXII)

Since the correspondence between Rivers and Adeline generally expresses mutual dissatisfaction, these letters can be correctly interpreted only in the light of those written to and by Rivers' other friends, which alert the reader that the lovers are concealing a great deal and even misrepresenting a few things. The story, then, is organically suited not only to the letter-novel, but more exactly to this particular variant: Crébillon's Marquise and her lover, or Fanni Butlerd and hers, are capable of declaring their love and sorting out their own feelings, but Rivers and Adeline are not, so their own letters are not sufficient to bring them together.

Although there are only four active correspondents, the impression of a broader exchange is given by continual references to material which the real reader never sees. In addition to Cardigan, whose letters do not appear, at least half a dozen other "silent" correspondents are mentioned. In a letter to Adeline, for example, Rivers remarks, "Je vous envoie une lettre de Milady Falmouth; elle se trompe, comme vous le verrez, puisqu'elle me croit de l'influence sur votre cœur. Ma réponse l'assure de sa méprise" (XXIX). Neither Lady Falmouth's letter nor Rivers' response is produced, and no further clues are given to her identity. At other moments, Rivers mentions letters which Cardigan has quoted to him, and which are thus twice removed from the real reader. He even attempts, now and again, to prevent a letter which is projected for the future from coming into existence: "Tu m'effraies en m'annonçant une lettre de Sir George. Il veut m'écrire, et d'où vient donc? Il m'obligera fort s'il se dispense de ce soin" (II). In addition to the forty-six letters comprising the body of the novel, there are numerous "copies" of letters which are included in other letters. In several instances, though, the "copied" letters are unreasonably long, or else they have been copied and forwarded for no discernible purpose except to apprise the novel's reader of what is transpiring. On one occasion Rivers includes in a letter to Adeline a packet of letters sent to him by her sister, Lady Lesley; it contains copies of three letters written to Lady Lesley and her husband by Adeline herself, along with copies of the responses. The obvious question is why Rivers takes the trouble of sending to Adeline copies of letters which she herself originally composed and with which she is therefore familiar. His explanation is that he wishes to impress his pupil with the disrespect she has shown her sister: "Je mets le tout sous vos yeux, dans l'espoir qu'en voyant vos propres expressions retracées de la main de Lady Lesley, vous vous étonnerez qu'elles soient échappées à votre plume" (XVI). If he does not also explain the presence of the copies of the two letters which Adeline has already received from her sister, it is presumably because all the copies had been integrated by Lady Lesley into her own letter to Rivers; he is simply sending everything along as he received it, rather than recopying and editing. (His plan, incidentally, is unsuccessful: Adeline refuses to waste her time rereading letters of which she is either the author or the original addressee.)

The inclusion of the Adeline-Lady Lesley correspondence within Rivers' letters to Adeline, however unrealistic it may seem, does allow for the expression of a multiplicity of viewpoints regarding Adeline, while safeguarding the position of Rivers at the novel's center. (With the exception of the last letter of the novel, all the letters are written either by Rivers or to him; letters between Adeline and her sister are subordinated to Rivers because they appear only as he incorporates them into his correspondence.) But this widening of the focus does not result from the kind of novel which *Lettres de Mylord Rivers* is, since in any single-writer letter-novel the protagonist can quote the letters of someone else and thus provide a new point of view. Only when both sides of a situation are presented directly by two different writers, are we face to face with the originality of the "polyphonic" letter-novel. This is the situation in a discussion between Rivers and Lady Mary. He sends her an account of the friendship between two Frenchwomen (who, indeed, rather resemble Mme Riccoboni and her friend Thérèse Biancolelli); their attitudes he finds noble and their conduct exemplary. Lady Mary comments, "Je l'ai trouvé très long, très froid ... Madame de Chazèle est une bonne femme, de caractère assez insipide; et votre Comtesse, si sensible, si raisonnable, est à mes yeux la plus folle des créatures" (XXVII). What was interpreted by Rivers as sublime is seen by her as ridiculous. The next to last letter provides another example of the technique of multiple vantage points. Adressed to Rivers by Lady Orrery, it speaks of the love between Rivers and Adeline, but it tells from Adeline's point of view what the reader until now has seen mainly through the eyes of Rivers. The light which it throws on the situation brings about the dénouement: once Lady Orrery has made Rivers appreciate Adeline's position and recognize her love for him, he hurries to her side, thereby terminating both the Paris visit and his correspondence.

This last of Mme Riccoboni's novels has a charming and rather curious character, for she assumes an attitude toward her work which is to be found in none of the earlier novels. Several passages read like a commentary on the part of an amused author who cannot help smiling at her effort to present fiction as though it were reality. For example, Lady Mary, after severely criticizing the story of the two Frenchwomen, terminates her remarks with the following apology: "Pardon, Mylord, j'oubliais que ce petit roman est une histoire" (XXVII). There is a certain similarity between Lady Mary and more especially Lady Orrery, on the one hand, and on the other Mme Riccoboni herself at this point in her life: these two characters appear as relatively disabused women whose experience and dispassion offset the youth and idealism of Adeline and Rivers. The two latter are, moreover, treated with a kind of pleasant irony; their petulance and misunderstandings are not viewed as tragic or deplorable — as they would have been in the earlier Riccoboni novels — but are seen rather as a kind of diverting spectacle, and Rivers and Adeline themselves as silly children. When Lady Orrery decides at the novel's end to tell Rivers in no uncertain terms how things stand, she does so, she declares, because she finds it necessary to "me débarrasser d'une espèce d'arbitrage entre deux grands enfants" (XLV). The story is brought to a speedy conclusion, then, when the two women tire of playacting and resolve to precipitate the happy ending — which was of course at no point in the novel in doubt [16]; Lady Mary announces to Rivers:

> Plus j'y songe, plus il me paraît que nous sommes un peu grands pour jouer à la climusette. Depuis longtemps vous clignez, Miss Rutland se cache, moi je triche en vous faisant des signes équivoques. L'amusement est bien uniforme au moins, il me lasse et je vous avertis que je ne suis plus du jeu. (XLIV)

Mme Riccoboni was over sixty when she published *Lettres de Mylord Rivers,* and had already confided to Garrick several years earlier that she felt a trifle old to busy herself with imagining love stories:

> Faire encore des romans, toujours parler d'amour, de sentiment, de passion! Je suis bien grande pour m'occuper de ces propos enfantins; le temps où j'aimais est si loin de moi! Quand je m'applique à peindre les transports de deux jeunes amants il me semble que je radote. (N. 52)

This attitude helps to explain not only the amused detachment which shows up in *Lettres de Mylord Rivers,* but the format as well. A letter-novel to which several writers contribute allows the love interest to be relegated at times to a position of secondary importance, and provides a suitable vehicle for the development of a philosophy of life and art side by side with the requisite love story.

This novel is as distinct in Mme Riccoboni's career as was her first, and for the same basic reason — each is well adapted to the form in which it is written; that is to say that in neither case could

---

[16] As the *Correspondence littéraire* remarked, "Le dénouement est prévu presqu'aussitôt que l'action commence à se développer" (XI [October 1776], 361).

the same story be told so effectively in any other way. Just as the number, disposition and tone of Fanni's letters reveal and, moreover, influence her emotional state, so do the letters which pass between Rivers and his friends throw different lights on his relationship with Adeline while they actually serve to modify that relationship. Both novels are free of the abductions, fortuitous coincidences and surprises which occur in some of the other works: the story here *is* the correspondence. *Lettres de Fanni Butlerd* is by far the better of the two, for its simplicity and vitality, and for the sincerity and immediacy of the emotions it describes; but *Lettres de Mylord Rivers* is notable as an example of a well-orchestrated letter-novel, and its interest is closely related to that fact.

Chapter V

THE EGOCENTRIC MALE

> Ils aiment, disent-ils! Tromper l'objet de ses désirs, lui préparer de longs regrets, l'avilir, le livrer à la douleur, à la honte! est-ce aimer? Eh, que seraient-ils donc s'ils haïssaient?
>
> *Histoire de Miss Jenny*

The portrait of the male which emerges from a reading of the novels of Mme Riccoboni is neither complete nor detailed, and this is in part a result of the perspective of the novels. In all but one of the epistolary works, the correspondence of the woman alone appears and the reader has access to the man's words only insofar as they are quoted in her letters; thus it is exclusively through the eyes of the female that men are viewed. For the most part, Mme Riccoboni is interested in men only in their relations with women: it is the sensibilities, tribulations and destiny of the heroine which principally concern her. Even in the two non-letter novels *(Histoire du Marquis de Cressy* and *Histoire d'Ernestine)*, the point of view remains essentially feminine and the narrator, who identifies closely with the cause of the female characters, is far from objective. Women, for example, are referred to as "nous."

The central idea of these novels — with the exception of *Lettres de Mylord Rivers,* which is an anomaly in Mme Riccoboni's literary productions — was well defined in an unsigned 1841 article in the *Revue de Paris:*

> Que l'artifice, l'égoïsme, l'ambition, la légèreté d'un homme, peuvent conduire au désespoir la femme paisible,

heureuse, belle et brillante avant d'aimer; la conduire au mépris des biens que le monde estime, au mépris de la beauté, de la jeunesse, de la naissance, de la richesse, au mépris des plaisirs, au mépris de la vie.[1]

For the way they treat women, Mme Riccoboni makes an attack on men which is eloquent and at times vituperative; she indicts them, along with those elements in society which uphold them, on a variety of counts. Probably the fault most commonly imputed to them is an overriding sensuality: they have no understanding of the true nature of love, so that the only aspect of the experience which has any meaning for them is the sensual. This refrain is heard over and again: "Esclaves de leur sens, lorsqu'ils le paraissent être de nos charmes," writes Juliette Catesby, "c'est pour eux qu'ils nous cherchent, qu'ils nous servent; ils ne considèrent en nous que les plaisirs qu'ils espèrent de goûter par nous" (XXII). This opinion seems to have prevailed in Mme Riccoboni's mind as far back as the composition of the *Suite de Marianne;* she has her Marianne qualify men as "de faibles créatures dont la grandeur d'âme et la force prétendue ne résistent jamais au caprice, à la passion, à la plus légère impulsion de leurs sens."[2] So limited, in fact, is men's concept of love that they are incapable of comprehending what the same phenomenon signifies for woman: "L'attachement d'une femme délicate est au-dessus des idées de votre sexe: vous ne connaissez qu'une preuve de notre amour; vous ignorez combien est fort le sentiment qui nous conduit à vous la donner" (*Lettres de Fanni Butlerd,* XCVII). The essential difference between men and women is that for the former, the physical aspect of love is endowed with an independent importance, whereas for the latter, a physical relationship is the result of a strong moral and psychological commitment and has meaning only in the light of that commitment.

The male protagonists themselves recognize their sensual character and readily admit that they are inferior in this regard to women; even Mylord Rivers owns that "un homme est une faible créature, moins capable que vous, peut-être, de résister à

---

[1] Mme M., "Mme Riccoboni," *Revue de Paris,* 35 (1841), 202.
[2] *La Vie de Marianne,* p. 616.

l'impulsion de ses sens, d'arrêter la fougue de ses désirs" (X). Such avowal, however, is usually made only in order to guarantee themselves the right to make mistakes — a right which they deny to women. Men allow themselves failings on the side of sensuality because, they say, the masculine heart and senses do not necessarily act in unison. A man expects, therefore, that he has only to repent of his faults for them to be forgiven; "soyez sûre," says Juliette Catesby, "qu'il se procurera des occasions de se repentir" (VII). She later lambasts men for their inconsistent reasoning in this regard:

> par ces distinctions qu'ils prennent pour excuse, ils se réservent la faculté d'être excités par l'amour, séduites par la volupté, ou entraînés par *l'instinct*.... Mais cette excuse qu'ils prennent, ils ne la reçoivent pas; remarquez cela: ce qu'ils séparent en eux, ils le réunissent en nous. (XXXVI)

This is part of the insidious double standard against which Mme Riccoboni inveighs: a man's errors are always forgotten but a woman's dishonor her for life. Fanni Butlerd alludes to this double standard when she explains that a man does not suffer at the end of a love affair, while his partner pays the price of lasting shame: "Trahi, quitté, haï de ce qu'il aime, un homme peut toujours se rappeler avec plaisir le temps où il se trouvait heureux... Mais nous... nous joignons au regret de perdre notre bonheur la honte de l'avoir goûté" (XV). If, then, men acknowledge feminine superiority, it is in order to demand more of women than they ask of themselves; because of the woman's natural goodness and righteousness, no indulgence is granted to her:

> Si l'extrême violence de cette passion est l'excuse d'un sexe porté par son éducation, par sa hardiesse naturelle, à ne pas contraindre ses désirs, à sacrifier beaucoup au plaisir de les satisfaire, la retenue et la modération, partage ordinaire du nôtre, ne lui donnent point de droit à la même indulgence: c'est un combat inégal, ma chère, où l'on impose au plus timide, au plus faible, la nécessité de remporter la victoire. (*Lettres de Sophie de Vallière*, XVIII)

Ironically, men make extraordinary demands of courage and strength on the sex which they nonetheless scornfully regard as physically the weaker, and whose weakness they simultaneously exploit for their own selfish ends: "L'art difficile de résister, de vaincre ses penchants, de maîtriser la nature même fut laissé par eux au sexe qu'ils traitent de faible, qu'ils osent mépriser comme faible" (*Lettres de Juliette Catesby*, XXII). In an unequal encounter with men, women are expected, by their moral force, to be the victors.

The situation is all the more unjust because of the authority which men exercise. They use their power in society in order to maintain women in a subordinate position. This involves a strange and subtle contradiction in their attitude, because while they style themselves the guardians and benefactors of womankind, it is they alone who continually bring to ruin those they pretend to protect. Henriette, a vocal and disabused spinster in *Histoire d'Ernestine*, assures the young heroine that men "se prétendent formés pour guider, soutenir, protéger, un sexe *faible* et *timide*: cependant eux seuls l'attaquent, entretiennent sa timidité, et profitent de sa faiblesse" (p. 57). Men establish a code ostensibly intended for the preservation of women's honor, yet they continually encourage, even constrain, individual women to violate the code. Henriette explains the workings of the system: with regard to how men treat women, she comments, "ils leur ont imposé des devoirs, ils leur donnent des lois, et par une bizarrerie révoltante, née de l'amour d'eux-mêmes, ils les pressent de les enfreindre, et tendent des pièges à ce sexe *faible, timide*, dont ils osent se dire le conseil et l'appui" (p. 57). Men therefore enjoy the privilege of being at the same time lawmakers and tempters. It is the same contradiction between what men demand in groups, setting norms, and what they require individually of women, which results in the unfortunate plight of illegitimate children, the results of men's egotistical desire to satisfy their senses. The heroine of *Histoire de Miss Jenny*, herself illegitimate, delivers an eloquent condemnation of laws which discriminate against the guiltless while the real criminals are left unpunished:

> quel préjugé faux et barbare soumet au mépris tant d'innocentes créatures, et laisse jouir de l'estime publique

les auteurs du crime dont elles subissent la honte! Nos pères ont établi des lois bien injustes. L'intérêt les conserve en vigueur, l'amour du plaisir les enfreint sans cesse. Quelle contrariété dans nos principes et dans nos mœurs! (Part II, pp. 18-19) [3]

Add to men's sensuality a host of other faults, including selfishness, ambition and faithlessness, and the result is that what they call love often becomes the abuse of women. The object of a man's desires is more likely to suffer than to benefit from the honor. To such an extent is this true that his love is sometimes indistinguishable in its effects from his hate: "Que les hommes sont inconséquents et cruels ... Ils aiment, disent-ils! Tromper l'objet de ses désirs, l'avilir, le livrer à la douleur, à la honte, est-ce aimer? Eh, que seraient-ils donc s'ils haïssaient?" (*Histoire de Miss Jenny*, part II, p. 93). Even the most well-meaning of men, because of their fundamental moral debility, may bring only one trial after another to the women they love.

* * *

In a letter to Choderlos de Laclos, Mme Riccoboni wrote, "Un homme extrêmement pervers est aussi rare dans la société qu'un homme extrêmement vertueux" (April 19, 1782). Her novels reflect this opinion: if there are few totally upstanding men in these works, neither are there many full-fledged villains. The majority of them are not all bad: egotistical and weak-willed, they nonetheless have some better instincts, even if they do manage too often to suppress them. Antoine-François Riccoboni, the author's husband, was himself a strange combination of good will and vices, and could have been the model for the male protagonists of some of the novels; just after his death, his widow described him to David Garrick in these terms: "Il semblait avoir étudié l'art de se nuire à lui-même et de désespérer les autres. Non qu'il fût méchant, mais il était fou ... Il m'avait rendue

---

[3] Cf. the story of Polly Baker in Diderot's *Supplément au Voyage de Bougainville* for a reflection from a masculine viewpoint on the same intrinsic social injustice.

malheureuse, et pourtant il m'estimait beaucoup, et même m'aimait à sa manière" (N. 91).

In the novels, the Marquis de Cressy is the archetype of this breed of man, and is drawn in greater detail than other male figures. His character has been aptly described by Joachim Merlant: "c'est la légèrté impulsive dans les affaires du cœur, agravée d'une ambition logique et implacable, qui conduit le marquis ... mais le premier élan est bon, l'instinct pur et clair de la conscience ne l'aurait pas trahi s'il l'avait écouté." [4] Never completely antipathetic, Cressy is nonetheless "toujours lamentable d'indécision et de lâcheté." [5] He repeatedly stifles the promptings of his better self and gives rein to his vices, but each time he succumbs to temptation his conscience makes itself heard, so that Cressy never entirely enjoys the fruits of his wickedness.

Histoire de Monsieur le Marquis de Cressy, which was published in 1758 — one year after *Lettres de Fanni Butlerd* — is a brief and absorbing novel which details the process by which a fundamentally well-intentioned man, dominated by sensuality, ambition and vanity, brings to ruin at least three women. The portrait of the male which appears at the beginning of the novel is illustrative of Mme Riccoboni's gift for evoking the salient characteristic of her protagonists with rapidity, concision, and grace:

> Il était maître de lui-même; assez riche, si ses désirs eussent été modérés; mais dominé par l'ambition, le bien de ses pères ne pouvait suffire à l'état qu'il avait pris; il songea à le soutenir, même à l'augmenter; une grande naissance, une figure charmante, mille talents, une humeur complaisante, l'air doux, le cœur faux, beaucoup de finesse dans l'esprit, l'art de cacher ses vices et de connaître le faible d'autrui, fondaient ses espérances; elles ne furent point déçues. (P. 2)

The first of a series of vacillations on Cressy's part occurs when he discovers that sixteen-year-old Adélaïde du Bugei is in love

---

[4] *Le Roman personnel de Rousseau à Fromentin* (Paris: Hachette, 1905), p. 4.
[5] André Monglond, *Le Préromantisme français* (Grenoble, 1930), I, 229.

with him. Genuinely fond of her, Cressy is all the same aware that she is not wealthy enough to be a very good match:

> Il sentit un plaisir secret en observant l'impression qu'il faisait sur ce cœur simple et vrai; mais comme il était fort éloigné de borner son ambition à la fortune qu'elle pouvait lui apporter, il rejeta d'abord toute idée de profiter des dispositions d'Adélaïde: mais le temps, la vanité, le désir, l'amour peut-être, détruisirent cette sage résolution, et lui présentèrent un moyen d'entretenir le goût que mademoiselle du Bugei lui laissait voir, sans rien changer au plan qu'il s'était déjà formé pour son élévation. (P. 6)

Indicative of Cressy's good side are his capacity to be touched by a love which is simple and true and his initial resolution to act honorably; but his sensual nature proves too powerful for him and he resolves to take advantage of the penchant which Adélaïde naively allowed him to perceive. From here on, Cressy's behavior is a sequence of hesitations, and at each step, in anticornelian fashion, he eventually chooses the less admirable option. Each time he falters he is saddened by his conduct, but never to the extent of correcting it. But while Cressy is destroying Adélaïde, he is also forfeiting his peace of mind.

It is notable that Cressy becomes attracted to Adélaïde only *after* he realizes her inclination for him; this is a pattern of behavior which will remain constant throughout the novel. Too irresolute, too debilitated perhaps, ever to initiate romance, Cressy simply allows himself to be loved; he responds to the overtures of several women and becomes the passive recipient of their affections. When he fortuitously discovers that a wealthy young widow, Mme de Raisel, is also in love with him, he promptly banishes Adélaïde from his mind, courts and wins the widow. Soon after the marriage, he becomes involved in a love affair with a young protégée of his wife, Hortense de Berneil — one of the rare unworthy female figures in the works of Mme Riccoboni. Interestingly, it is not Cressy's merits which attract Hortense, but rather the fact of his being loved by a virtuous woman: "l'ardeur avec laquelle il était aimé l'embellissait à ses yeux" (p. 97). The interplay between Cressy and Hortense constitutes one of the most convincing psychological studies in Mme Riccoboni's novels: neither is genuinely fond of the other, but for each the challenge is impossible to resist. Jealous of the happiness of Mme de Raisel, Hortense becomes passionately committed to having Cressy for her own.

When Mme de Raisel discovers the duplicity of her husband, she decides to commit suicide. She makes her preparations with calm, drinks a cup of poison which she contrives to receive from her husband's hands, and dies in his arms, expressing her forgiveness of both him and Hortense. Mme de Raisel's suicide precedes that of Goethe's Werther by sixteen years; it even precedes by several years the long discussions on suicide which appear in the correspondence between Saint-Preux and Milord Edouard in *La Nouvelle Héloïse:* the Riccoboni heroine would seem to be one of the earliest fictional characters to kill herself for love.[6] After her benefactors's death, Hortense is filled with remorse and enters a convent. Cressy himself, like a Prévostian hero, spends the remainder of his days in repentence, haunted by the specters of the women he brought to ruin: "M. de Cressy ne put se consoler; Adélaïde sacrifiée pour lui, madame de Raisel morte dans ses bras, formèrent un tableau qui, se représentant sans cesse à son idée, empoisonna le reste de ses jours" (p. 146).

This combination of good and bad qualities, though more finely drawn in Cressy than elsewhere, is characteristic of other male figures in these novels. Danby is of a similar ilk. An impassioned young man who tricks the heroine of the *Histoire de Miss Jenny* into believing that he has married her, he does so out of genuine though misdirected affection for the young lady. Already wedded to an older woman, Danby pretends to marry Jenny in the expectation that his wife's death will soon leave him free to act honorably toward the girl. Like most men, he is lacking in

---

[6] The episode did not fail to raise a few eyebrows: *L'Année littéraire* objected to Mme de Raisel's suicide on the grounds that "on lui trouve l'âme trop vertueuse et les passions trop douces pour la faire finir par ce genre de mort" (1758, IV, 128); this is the suicide which so horrified Mme de Genlis, who wrote, "Mme Riccoboni a eu la première la funeste idée de vouloir rendre le suicide intéressant, et c'est un reproche grave que l'on doit faire à sa mémoire. Il n'est permis d'attribuer cet acte affreux qu'à un personnage vicieux et perverti" (*De l'Influence des femmes sur la littérature française,* p. 280).

discretionary powers and his judgment is clouded by his selfishness. He is incapable of comprehending the extent to which he wrongs Jenny, for he has no idea how fragile a possession is woman's honor and with what care it must be treated. As a woman, Jenny's position is such that a crime to which she in no way acquiesced destroys her dignity and self-esteem. Having escaped from Danby, she laments,

> Je ne trouve plus en moi cette dignité, ce sentiment intérieur, qui au milieu de mes peines, dans le sein de la pauvreté, m'élevait à mes propres yeux. Hélas! qu'est-il devenu? Comment le crime de cet homme me réduit-il à la honte, à l'abaissement, à n'oser fixer mes regards sur les autres, à rougir en les tournant sur moi-même? (Part III, p. 16)

Once again the double standard comes into play, and Jenny pays the price of Danby's crime while he continues to enjoy society's respect.

One of the characteristics which Cressy and Danby have in common — their penchant for dissimulation — is found in its most malignant state in the first husband of Mme de Sancerre. We learn about Sancerre, who has been dead for several years when the novel opens, through what his widow writes to her correspondent, the Comte de Nancé:

> Dès sa plus tendre jeunesse, monsieur de Sancerre s'était étudié à déguiser ses penchants, à paraître différent de lui-même; sans principes, sans âme, intéressé, faux, ingrat, la dissimulation et la finesse furent les seules qualités qu'il jugea nécessaire d'acquérir et de perfectionner. (*Lettres de Madame de Sancerre*, XVI)

Men who simulate passion are common in the sentimental novel [7]; only after her marriage did Mme de Sancerre discover that her husband's love for her was feigned and his courtship motivated by the prospect of financial gain. Outwardly his conduct toward

---

[7] In Crébillon's *Heureux Orphelins* (1754), the Duchess of Suffolck exclaims, "Grand Dieu! pourquoi faut-il que les hommes puissent jouer si facilement la passion et les mouvements qui peuvent en indiquer une, ou que nous soyions assez malheureuses pour les en croire pénétrés sur des marques si faibles et si peu sûres?" (*Œuvres* [Londres, 1779], V, 129).

her remained exemplary, but in private he treated her with indifference or even cruelty. This recalls Marivaux's analyses of social masks: in *Le Jeu de l'amour et du hasard* Silvia asks "Les hommes ne se contrefont-ils pas, surtout quand ils ont de l'esprit?" She goes on to speak of a man who appears all charm in public and adds:

> Oui, fiez-vous-y à cette physionomie si douce, si prévenante, qui disparaît un quart d'heure après, pour faire place à un visage sombre, brutal, farouche, qui devient l'effroi de toute une maison! Ergaste s'est marié; sa femme, ses enfants, son domestique, ne lui connaissent encore que ce visage-là, pendant qu'il promène partout ailleurs cette physionomie si aimable que nous lui voyons, et qui n'est qu'un masque qu'il prend au sortir de chez lui. (Act I, Scene 1)

So effectively did Sancerre play the role of loving and tender husband that his wife was universally judged as bizarre and capricious for eventually leaving him; and even after his death, society continues to misprize her, but only because she nobly refuses to justify herself by revealing to anyone (except her confidant) what had been his true character. This is a common theme in the Riccoboni novels: the world repeatedly misjudges women because it fails to appreciate the extent of men's duplicity. When the woman does react against the ill treatment of her husband, she is never understood and generally is condemned as insensitive to his fine qualities. Women are all the more incapable of dealing with this state of affairs in that they themselves are inherently sincere and straightforward. Like Fanni Butlerd, they are chiefly concerned with honesty at any price: "Je veux toujours être vraie, dussé-je vous fâcher" (LXXIII). Like her, they could not deceive if they wanted to: "le cœur que vous aviez touché," she tells Alfred, "n'est pas capable d'une longue contrainte, et lorsqu'il veut dissimuler, ses plus grands efforts lui sont inutiles" (CXIV). Mme de Sancerre likewise declares "Je n'ai point l'art de feindre: j'ai dédaigné cet art trop utile dans la société. Mes yeux expriment tous les mouvements de mon âme" (XXVII). There is little doubt that men's fraud is the most reprehensible of their faults: "toute dissimulation est une perfidie" (*Lettres de Sophie de Vallière*, XLIII).

While Sancerre probably represents masculinity at its worst, there are several examples of men who are not completely blameworthy. The most admirable of Mme Riccoboni's male figures is Mylord Rivers, created when her own husband was deceased and she herself older and perhaps less impassioned in her approach. But earlier in her career, she had described three male figures in whom the good outweighs the bad: Ossery, Clémengis and Germeuil — the suitors respectively of Juliette Catesby, Ernestine and Sophie de Vallière. But, significantly, in spite of his good traits, none of the three is entirely exempt from the major defects of his sex. Let us first consider Clémengis, to whom more pages are devoted than to either of the other two.

Histoire d'Ernestine (1765) is a short and engaging narrative about how a poor orphan of undistinguished birth, who earns a precarious living by painting miniatures, marries a marquis. From the start, the Marquis de Germeuil is presented as superior to the average male; one of the most telling indicators of his goodness is that, unlike most men, he has no gift for feigning. On the contrary, he is "peu accoutumé à déguiser les penchants de son âme" (p. 75). Ernestine's friend Henriette, a spinster whose vast experience has given her the lowest opinion of men — recognizes in Clémengis an exceptional character:

> la noble franchise de monsieur de Clémengis, sa générosité, un amour si tendre, si désintéressé, lui paraissait un sentiment nouveau; le grand monde où elle vivait depuis son enfance ne lui en avait jamais donné l'idée. (P. 70)

Charmed with Ernestine's talents and innocence, Clémengis buys her a house, stocks it with books and music, provides her with tutors and encourages her to cultivate her natural gifts. Although he is in love with her, Clémengis acts disinterestedly and asks nothing of his young protégée except friendship. The two live a kind of idyll until Henriette discovers the situation and determines to point out to Ernestine the risks she has been running; she declares that while the intentions of Clémengis may not be evil, he is nonetheless ill advised in endangering Ernestine's reputation, since in the eyes of the world there can be only a single explanation for his largesse.

Of all the Riccoboni heroines Ernestine is the least worldly-wise and the most oblivious of conventional mores; until now blissfully unaware of the dangers of commerce with men, she finds that knowledge is painful and wishes that Henriette had never enlightened her:

> Ah! fallait-il m'éclairer! mon erreur me rendait si heureuse! que je hais le monde, ses usages, ses préjugés, ses malignes observations! que dois-je à ce monde où je ne vis point? quoi! faudra-t-il immoler mon bonheur à ses fausses opinions? eh! que m'importe ses vains, ses téméraires jugements, quand je suis innocente, quand mon cœur ne se reproche rien? (P. 60)

Happiness, Ernestine discovers (as do most of them sooner or later), is based largely upon ignorance or illusion and therefore continually threatened. In spite of her expressed contempt for society's opinion, Ernestine's joy at being with the Marquis is dissipated and the spontaneity which formerly existed between them is altogether banished from their conversation. By now deeply in love, Clémengis even considers renouncing his inheritance and marrying her; he hesitates, though, out of regard for Ernestine's happiness, fearful that one day he may be weak enough to blame her for his loss of fortune and position. Ironically, his superiority resides partly at least in his recognition of his limitations: realizing that men are prone to inconstancy in their opinions and affections, he wishes to protect Ernestine from this facet of the male character. But even he is too much a male for his good qualities and laudable resolutions to predominate forever; sensuality and egotism eventually get the upper hand. Just as the Marquis de Cressy determines to seduce Adélaïde when he decides not to marry her, so Clémengis, having resolved not to ask for Ernestine's hand, subtly pressures her to settle for a less formal bond. In her disingenuous fashion, Ernestine is extremely clever: she agrees to do anything for the man she loves, but in her very insistence on her willingness to forfeit both self-esteem and reputation, she makes Clémengis feel the weight of the sacrifice he is asking. Shamed and touched by her devotion, he repents; the story ends happily: the lovers are wed and to boot the inheritance of the Marquis is secured.

The good qualities of the Marquis de Germeuil, suitor of Sophie de Vallière, likewise outnumber the bad. His defects may be summed up in his lack of perspicacity, which makes him incapable of really understanding the fair sex, and lack of moderation, which makes him at times dangerous to woman. Ossery, in *Lettres de Juliette Catesby*, is in a sense more interesting than either Clémengis or Germeuil because, while their inclinations to immoderacy are held in check, his are not: in a moment of drunken abandon he seduces the sister of a friend. For Ossery, of course, there seems to be no contradiction in being devoted to one woman and physically attracted to another. But he at least has the strength of character to marry the girl whose honor he has compromised and, after her death, returns to be forgiven and is reinstated in the good graces of Juliette.

The role in which these male characters are most frequently cast is, obviously, that of seducer — or rather would-be seducer because, significantly, few of them succeed. The heroines seldom succumb to the male's urgings and in those instances when they do, they are willing to accept complete responsibility for their actions.[8] Nothing like the long and close analysis of seduction which occurs in the novels of Richardson and Laclos is to be found here, because Mme Riccoboni is more interested in the effects on the woman than in the method of the seducer. Neither is there any of the ritual of quasi seduction found in most of Crébillon's novels, which is of no interest to Mme Riccoboni.[9] But the male assault in her novels is not different in its essentials from that described by them.

The aggressor begins by attempting to convince the woman of his undying love, and then tries to prompt her to reciprocate; he must move cautiously at this early stage, and seek to elicit love before she becomes aware of his designs. His task is rendered easier when she is young and naive, and therefore initially

---

[8] In this they differ from most of Crébillon's characters, with the notable exception of Fanni Butlerd's model, the Marquise de M***: "Il n'a point dépendu de moi de ne pas vous aimer ... mais il dépend de moi d'être vertueuse, et l'on ne cesse pas de l'être malgré soi" (*Lettres de la marquise*, p. 59).

[9] See chapter on Crébillon fils in Philip Stewart, *Le Masque et la parole* (Paris: José Corti, 1973).

unsuspecting both of the dangers of love and of the depravity of men. The orphaned girl is especially well suited to this particular fictional situation because of her lack of parental counsel. She has, like Marivaux's Marianne (and even like Pamela who, though not orphaned, is physically separated from her parents), no one to guide and instruct her in a moment of crisis; thus, she is that much more susceptible to all manner of accident and adventure, and to the wiles of the crafty male. Sophie de Vallière, Jenny and Ernestine accordingly are all orphans. Adélaïde du Bugei in *Histoire du marquis de Cressy* is not, but because her father is a weak figure, she, like the others, must fend for herself. Her plight, in fact, makes manifest the contrast between the approach of the young innocent and the more experienced woman: sixteen-year-old Adélaïde is in love with Cressy, as is a widowed countess of twenty-six. Both remain silent about their feelings for a long time, but for different reasons: "La comtesse gardait son secret par prudence, et Mlle du Bugei ignorait qu'elle en eût un à confier" (p. 5). Adélaïde's ignorance, like that of Ernestine, is in the tradition of the Princesse de Clèves, whose mother is aware long before she of her love for the Duc de Nemours — except that here the watchful mother is not present to warn her. Before Adélaïde makes the discovery of her love, Cressy himself "s'aperçut du désordre où la jetait sa présence et connut le penchant de son cœur" (p. 6). This is of course a major advantage for him.

Once signs of love have been ascertained, she must next be pressed to acknowledge her feelings; such an avowal, he will insist, is all that he needs to make him happy. The function of the letter may be a vital one here, since the woman is often more likely to acknowledge her feelings on paper than in person. This accomplished, he of course then declares that his happiness and peace of mind actually depend on her demonstrating that she loves him. After urging Fanni Butlerd merely to admit her love and thereby make him eternally happy, Alfred increases his demands; as she writes, "Vous m'avez promis de la reconnaissance, et vous en manquez déjà; m'écrire que je ne vous aime point, ou que je vous aime faiblement, c'est être ingrat" (XV). At this critical step, he makes an appeal to her sensibility, dramatically portraying her as the arbitrator of his happiness:

> Les hommes ont l'art de nous persuader que nous tenons leur bonheur entre nos mains. D'une idée si dangereuse, trop fortement imprimée dans nos âmes, naît cette pitié généreuse et cette tendre condescendance pour leurs désirs, que les ingrats nomment faiblesse quand elle cesse de les rendre heureux. (*Histoire de Miss Jenny*, part III, p. 48)

But if this tactic does not meet with immediate success, there are others at his disposal. He may, for example, deliberately excite her jealousy; Fanni capitulates just a few days after the discovery that Alfred spent an evening alone with another woman. Another conventional device is to arouse a woman's pity by means of real or feigned illness. Like Lovelace, and like the count in *Lettres de la marquise*, the suitors of Fanni Butlerd, Juliette Catesby, Sophie de Vallière and Ernestine all resort to this hackneyed method: each succeeds thereby in awakening the woman's concern and sympathy and at the same time encouraging her love to become manifest.

Fanni's reaction to the illness of the man she familiarly terms her "pauvre petit malade" (XIX) is typical: "Quelle nouvelle, mon cher Alfred! Je suis désolée. Que vais-je devenir? ... Mon Dieu, que mon inquiétude est vive! Comment cacher mon trouble, ma douleur, des pleurs qui m'échappent?" (XVIII). "Ah, cette maladie!" echoes Juliette Catesby, "où m'a-t-elle engagée?" (XXXIII). By allowing herself to voice her distress and fright, the woman begins to realize the extent of her commitment, and simultaneously accustoms herself to admitting and thereby increasing it; a man can better ascertain the strength of his position in the face of such acknowledgements. Juliette Catesby recognizes the workings of this system:

> Oh, ces hommes! ces hommes! Remarquez-vous comme ils savent tirer parti des événements? Lorsque les moyens de nous subjuguer semblent leur manquer, un incident imprévu, le hasard, une *maladie* les ramènent vers le but qu'ils s'étaient proposé. On ne veut point les voir; on ne veut point les entendre; tout paraît fini; mais leurs ressources ne s'épuisent jamais. Quand ils ne savent plus que faire, ils ont la fièvre, ma chère, ils n'ont plus qu'un instant à vivre. (XXXI)

However, Juliette demonstrates this kind of lucidity only after Ossery's recovery is complete and the damage to her heart is done; she concludes, moreover, by asking herself, "ses torts sont-ils diminués?" and answers, "non, mais... il a été *malade*."

Some men will go even further in an attempt to arouse pity: they may threaten to commit suicide. In *Histoire de Miss Jenny*, the young Comte d'Anglesey forces Jenny's friend to elope with him by writing her that if she refuses, she will soon discover that "ma main m'aura délivré d'une vie que vous seule pouviez me faire aimer" (part III, p. 78). The girl agrees, only to be rapidly deserted by him. But the suicide threat, altogether too sublime not to arouse cynicism among readers, is one of the most trite of the seduction devices in the sentimental novel and Mme Riccoboni resorts to it rarely.

All of the seduction attempts are characterized by two important factors, and when the man succeeds, it is chiefly owing to these. The first is his lack of self-respect and dignity, which makes him insensitive to the woman's displeasure and extraordinarily persistent in accomplishing his goal:

> Les hommes se lassent-ils des soins qu'ils prennent pour contenter leurs fantaisies? Ils ne se sentent point humiliés de nos refus: c'est encore un des avantages réservés à eux seuls.... [Un homme] s'embarrasse peu s'il cause de l'ennui, du dégoût; son âme n'est point assez délicate pour qu'il se trouve blessé de l'idée d'importuner. Occupé de lui seul, de ses intérêts, rien ne peut le faire renoncer au bien dont la possession le flatte. (*Lettres de Juliette Catesby*, XXIV)

Secondly, while his own shortcomings and insensitivity assist him in the perpetration of his designs, the woman's very superiority works in his favor too: she is too noble to imagine of what deception men are capable:

> Les hommes s'épargneraient la plus grande partie des peines qu'ils se donnent pour nous en imposer, s'ils pouvaient s'imaginer combien la noblesse de nos idées leur donne de facilité pour nous tromper. Une femme croirait se dégrader en supposant des vices à l'objet qu'elle a choisi pour celui de ses affections; et dès qu'elle aime,

elle accorde plus de vertus à son amant qu'il n'ose en feindre. (*Histoire du marquis de Cressy*, p. 64)

In the last analysis, it is the woman's goodness which eventually helps to bring about her downfall; her openness and honesty are too powerful to be suppressed, and that the man she loves should be unconvinced of her affections is a situation too painful to be tolerated. Adélaïde du Bugei's stance, when she is tempted to give in to the Marquis de Cressy, is typical: "Elle aimait, elle ne pouvait souffrir que son amant doutât de son amour" (p. 53). And Fanni Butlerd, after her fall, exclaims, "Mon cher amant est sûr que je l'aime; il ne doute plus de mes sentiments, je lui en ai donné la preuve la plus décidée" (XXXVII).

Seduction is not necessarily the greatest evil for the woman, however. When she has committed herself, happiness might still be within reach if man did not join to his duplicity and sensuality a third vice of his sex: inconstancy. These women know that the only thing really capable of maintaining constancy is the continual presence of obstacles; infidelity occurs as soon as all have been removed. Fanni Butlerd is sufficiently lucid to understand this; she writes, "Je sais que [le sacrifice que vous exigez] est sans prix pour celui qui le demande, l'espère, l'attend; mais trop souvent, dès qu'il est fait, dès que la victime est immolée, les fleurs qui la paraient se fanent, et l'on n'aperçoit plus en elle qu'un objet ordinaire" (XV). Fanni resorts to a rhetorical formula, "la victime immolée," to describe this sexist domination; yet, in spite of her disabused analysis of the situation, she does give in — and Alfred acts exactly as she had predicted.

This is, of course, a traditional view of men. In 1734, for her stage début as Lucile in Louis de Boissy's *La Surprise de la haine*, Mme Riccoboni had had to learn the following lines: "L'amour s'éteint toujours par la facilité: / Les grandes passions naissent des grands obstacles" (Act I, scene 5).[10] Time and again the penchant toward infidelity and the need for new conquests are seen as fundamental characteristics of men; for example, Mme de Selve in Duclos' *Confessions du comte de* ***, remarks, "Je vois

---

[10] Louis de Boissy, *La Surprise de la haine*, in *Œuvres* (Amsterdam and Berlin: Jean Neaulme, 1758), p. 120.

que la constance n'est pas au pouvoir des hommes, et leur éducation leur rend l'infidélité nécessaire." [11] In *Lettres de Mylord Rivers*, Lady Mary makes a similar observation to Rivers:

> Le cœur d'un homme, toujours en contradiction avec lui-même, n'est point formé pour goûter les charmes d'un commerce paisible. Il a besoin de craindre, d'espérer. Celle qui veut s'en rendre la maîtresse doit élever ses doutes, les dissiper, les faire renaître encore. L'inquiétude entretient l'activité de vos passions, elle seule bannit la langueur où vous jette la certitude de plaire. (XXVII)

While Mme Riccoboni's younger heroines, like Fanni Butlerd, usually intuit this, nevertheless an older friend will sometimes add the voice of experience to their own perceptions. Lady Charlotte, an acquaintance of Fanni Butlerd, counsels the same method as Lady Mary: "Il faut maîtriser, maltraiter un amant pour l'enchaîner, l'animer, le fixer" (LXXXVI). Mme Riccoboni's mature judgment and unhappy experience seem to speak through the mouths of Lady Charlotte and Lady Mary, but the heroines themselves are incapable of the artifice prescribed. In this respect they too resemble their creator, who wrote of herself in *L'Abeille* (the rather short-lived imitation of Addison's *Spectator* which she began in 1761), "tous mes sentiments se peignent sur mon front; je n'ai point l'art de me contraindre" (p. 229). So they generally disregard both instinct and advice; the result is that they often find themselves forsaken, and exclaiming like Juliette Catesby, "Qu'il est dur d'être abandonnée!"

* * *

The treatment of the battle between the sexes in the novels of Mme Riccoboni is, of course, in part based upon a social convention whereby men "attack" and women "defend" themselves as best they can. But while her contemporaries might view the woman's resistance as purely provisional and conventional, and her fundamental desires as similar to those of men, to Mme

---

[11] *Les Confessions du comte de* *** (1741), in *Romanciers du XVIII⁰ siècle*, II, 297.

Riccoboni there is an unbridgeable gap between the two combatants. She sees men, even those who are not thoroughgoing scoundrels, as inherently sensual creatures, while her heroines appear almost entirely devoid of carnal motive. By posing this basic dichotomy, she virtually rules out the possibility of any meaningful and long-term union between the sexes. At worst, the interaction with a male leaves the woman alone and disconsolate; at best, she may realize — after a series of difficulties and disappointments — a relatively satisfactory coexistence: this is the case for Ernestine, Sophie de Vallière and Juliette Catesby. But a real understanding and deep harmony between man and woman seem out of the question: Juliette may marry Ossery and attain a kind of fulfillment therein, but there must remain grave doubt that the delicate and introspective woman she is can find an authentic partner in the man she knows Ossery to be.

CHAPTER VI

WOMANHOOD: SENSE AND SENSIBILITY

> Une âme tendre est la source de toutes les peines d'une femme, la sensibilité est en elle un poison actif, que les soins d'un homme qui veut plaire, font fermenter, pour détruire son bonheur, égarer sa raison, et répandre l'amertume sur tous ses sentiments.
>
> *Lettres de Fanni Butlerd*
>
> Mon ami, il est bien peu de femmes dont on puisse envier le sort.
>
> *Lettres de Madame de Sancerre*

WOMEN IN LOVE

Love is the predominant theme in all of Mme Riccoboni's novels. Each of them is a novel of analysis, and since the protagonist is invariably someone in love, the object of analysis is in each case the dynamics and meaning of that experience. While the novels of contemporaries like Marivaux, Prévost and Challes are also often love stories, they have other dimensions as well, drawing as they frequently do on the texture of everyday life. Rousseau's *Nouvelle Héloïse* is at heart a love story, but it incorporates long dissertations on music, dueling, gardening, and so forth. Even Mme de Graffigny's *Lettres péruviennes* not only details the heroine's sentimental life, but also offers a critique of French society. Mme Riccoboni's novels are more limited in scope: except for *Lettres de Mylord Rivers*, where there is some philosophical content, these novels are not the vehicles for ideas on a wide variety of subjects; they are love stories and little else. There is no fabric of realism, either in décor or in the description of social classes, running through them, no discussion of art, of nature, or of civilization. The exclusive interest of the author is in the relations between the sexes. Here external description is reduced to a minimum and action is subordinate in importance to the psychology of the characters, most of whom are drawn from a society of relatively well-to-do people of leisure. Although thus limited, the analyses are refined and the evocation of the love experience is often both subtle and poignant.

Most of what Mme Riccoboni has to say about love is equally the consensus of the other novelists of the period, of Prévost, Duclos and Marivaux, for example; but in her works the picture is presented exclusively from the point of view of the woman author and the heroine. As a result, the emphasis, the nuances and the implications differ from theirs in some important respects. For one thing, Mme Riccoboni, unlike many novelists of the time, pays little attention to the sexual aspects of love; she is less interested in the external reality of physical love than in the sentimental phenomenon and the effects of loving on the woman's outlook. As she wrote to Liston in 1769:

> Il faut en croire Monsieur de Buffon. Il parle de l'amour en homme. *Le physique en est bon,* dit-il, *le moral n'en vaut rien.* Une femme aurait pensé tout le contraire. C'est ce moral qui nous occupe, nous attache, nous fait goûter des sensations bien plus délicieuses que ce *bon physique* de naturaliste. (N 51)

For another, she avoids portraying promiscuity: none of her heroines gives herself to a man without first committing herself psychologically; and their first love is generally also their last.

Fanni Butlerd and her successors are part of that elite for whom love is the only thing which matters. It is the sole pastime worthy of their concern, for they intuit that therein and therein alone must the sensitive woman conduct her search for happiness. But if there is no happiness without, love itself seldom brings lasting happiness: this paradox is at the base of Mme Riccoboni's novels. There is a constant tension between the desire for fulfillment in love and the futility of the hope — further emphasized in some cases by a presentiment of that futility. For these heroines, love is a necessary evil. Though it causes pain and anguish, they are helpless, even unwilling, to oppose it. "Comment est-il possible que notre cœur se donne?" asks Juliette Catesby, "Nous sommes si malheureuses en aimant!" (XXIV). In the letter just mentioned, where Mme Riccóboni contrasts the terms "physique" and "moral," she goes on to say,

> Il est la sauce du vrai bonheur, ce moral charmant! Pourquoi faut-il qu'il soit aussi la cause de toutes nos peines? Soyez-en sûr, mon ami, une personne sensible et délicate est rarement heureuse par le sentiment qu'elle éprouve, encore moins par celui qu'elle inspire. (N 51)

The most important factor in the predisposition of a woman toward love is, in fact, her *sensibilité:* "l'amour est la seule passion qui suffise entièrement à notre cœur" (*Histoire de Miss Jenny*, part I, p. 51). In the novels of Mme Riccoboni, as in most of those of the sentimental school, this gift is alternately eulogized and cursed — eulogized because the sensitive soul can know joy far beyond the ordinary, and cursed because one's capacity for suffering is proportionate to one's *sensibilité*. The guardian of young Sophie de Vallière thus pays her the highest compliment in terms which resemble an expression of pity: "Mais la pauvre petite! J'ai bien peur qu'elle ne soit un jour trop sensible" (III). What the lady really thinks is that although extreme *sensibilité* like Sophie's is not an unmixed blessing, one would not choose to have it diminished in the slightest. One of the women protagonists in *Histoire de Mylord Rivers,* Mylady d'Orrery, comments on the unreasonableness of this fatal inclination: "Mais d'où vient, mais pourquoi chérissons-nous tant cette sensation si contraire à notre repos? La sensibilité rendit-elle jamais une femme heureuse?" (IX). The answer to the latter question, as it appears in most of the novels of this author, is negative.

The interest of Mme Riccoboni's novels lies largely in her evocation of the mysterious genesis of love in the sensitive woman. For the birth of love in a woman's soul, she offers no rational explanation; it is an unaccountable reaction to a certain man, an event for which the woman has unknowingly been waiting, the end toward which her sensibility has always been directed. While falling in love obviously responds to a need within, there is nothing to explain why a given individual sets off the reaction; there seems to be a kind of psychological fatality at work. For the men whom these heroines do love are not exceptional; like the women themselves they are fairly ordinary people (except that "ordinary" for the male implies a host of defects). It is generally not a question of love at first sight, but rather of a spontaneous and subtle attraction which gradually develops into ardor, need and devotion.

Since the woman usually experiences love in almost total ignorance, she rarely understands at the outset what is happening, and is at first at a loss to interpret her feelings. That as a result of it she will eventually know pain and misery is not immediately evident. On the contrary, what is initially most striking about love is its extraordinary power: it appears as an overwhelming energy which embellishes every aspect of her life and being. She imagines herself a new person and the universe a miraculous place; her previously unhappy, or at best neutral existence seems suddenly metamorphosed into a state of euphoria. Out of emptiness and passivity emerge excitement, movement and the possibility of fulfillment. Nature seems to come to life and smile on her: "j'ai vu que l'amour animait tout, que tout semblait heureux par l'amour," says Mme de Sancerre (XXIII).

Love is accompanied by a wondrous discovery of unsuspected depths of experience; the heroine seems to shed her former self as she becomes capable of knowing great joy. A new and happier state seems to await her:

> quel mouvement rapide, senti pour la première fois, a porté jusqu'au fond de mon cœur une joie vive, un plaisir flatteur, un sentiment délicieux. Le souvenir de toutes mes peines s'est anéanti; l'idée de mon abaissement, de ma misère, s'est tout-à-coup effacé; il m'a semblé qu'on venait de me replacer dans un état heureux. (*Lettres de Sophie de Vallière*, XV)

In addition to this new awareness of herself as a potentially happy creature, there is a different perception of others, the discovery of beauty and delight in the world about her. As Juliette Catesby describes it:

> L'aveu d'un amour qu'on partage est un trait de lumière qui porte un nouveau jour dans nos idées. Un charme inconnu se répandit sur tout ce qui m'environnait; les objets changèrent à mes yeux, ils devinrent plus riants, plus aimables; je vis la nature s'embellir autour de moi. (XIV)

Love is an enchantment of the most powerful and the most pervasive kind; its effects are everywhere apparent. Falling in love, for Fanni Butlerd as for Juliette Catesby, changes the look and feel of everything:

> Un amant aimé embellit tout; il répand l'agrément dans les lieux qu'on habite, sur les personnes qu'on voit; il prête sa grâce à tous les objets qui nous environnent; le charme inexprimable attaché à sa présence semble s'étendre sur l'univers, et rendre tout plus aimable et plus riant. (LV)

In every instance, love creates a new world view in which the dominant elements are light, beauty and delectation.

Love is more than a revolution in terms of one's appreciation of persons and objects and of their potential for creating loveliness and joy. It further involves a new and unique grasp of notions which go beyond these: the experience of love brings an elastic sense of time and space. Matter and duration are no longer dealt with objectively; they take on different aspects according to the presence or absence of the loved one. For the woman, only those places count which have some significance in terms of him; Miss Jenny explains that, when we fall in love, "L'étendue de l'univers semble diminuer à nos yeux, et nous en apercevons seulement l'espace où se referment nos désirs" (part I, p. 95). Fanni Butlerd, as we have just seen, speaks of the "charme inexprimable" — the aura, so to speak — attached to Alfred's presence; wherever he has been, the charm lingers even after he is gone, and Fanni can tolerate only those localities which he has visited. From all the rest she is alienated: "Ma chambre est un pays étranger pour moi: je ne vous y ai jamais vu. Ici tout est vif, tout est riant, tout a reçu l'empreinte chérie: ce cabinet est mon univers" (XXI). While the woman experiences a concentration of space, and tends to neglect all those locations which have no association with the lover, time too seems to converge on his presence. Its ordinary rhythm is destroyed and there is a new perception of its passage: time flies when the lover is present and becomes insufferably slow when he is gone: "Je vous attends. Mes yeux sont fixés sur l'aiguille de ma montre; qu'elle va lentement! Dans deux heures elle volera; il me le semblera du moins..." (*Lettres de Fanni Butlerd*, XXIV). Miss Jenny too describes this phenomenon:

> Le temps cessa d'avoir pour moi une durée égale. Je trouvais les heures longues pendant le jour, elles s'écoulaient le soir avec une rapidité surprenante. Quand le Comte de Clare sortait, la vivacité dont je venais de me sentir animée, s'évanouissait." (Part IV, p. 62)

For Fanni, activity and animation are characteristic only of those instants when the lover is present; when he is not, "le jour paraît long; il dure, passe, finit, rien ne l'a marqué: il est anéanti, on ne se souvient pas qu'il a été: la vivacité, l'esprit, l'enjouement, ne peuvent passer le voile qui les obscurcit" (LV). One remembers exclusively those moments marked by his company, as one cares only about those places he has frequented.

While Mme Riccoboni's notion of love as the most prodigious and revolutionary of phenomena, and her association of movement, beauty, and happiness with love, are eloquently expressed, these are not original with her; more interesting perhaps is her conception of the origin of love's power. In these novels, the energy of love is always projected by the heroine: she is seen as the center from which it emanates. The male, as the more passive figure, is viewed as the object of love, never as its source. Only in the woman does love become a creative, revolutionizing force. Mme Riccoboni's heroines, amazed as they are by its marvelous powers, are nonetheless soon aware that it is within themselves that these powers are born. Even though she is physically the weaker, during the love affair the woman is, morally and psychologically, the stronger force.

All of these heroines have the insight and the lucidity to realize the omnipotence of their love. They know, for example, that a woman's love can itself seem to beautify its object. Of her admiration for Mylord d'Ossery, Juliette Catesby writes to her confidante,

> notre prévention fait tout le mérite de l'objet que nous préférons; elle pare l'idole de notre cœur; elle lui donne chaque jour un nouvel ornement. Peu à peu l'éclat dont nous l'avons revêtu nous éblouit nous-mêmes, nous en impose, nous séduit, et nous adorons follement l'ouvrage de notre imagination. (XXVI) [1]

Just as, by dint of writing about passion, a woman may come eventually to experience it in all the force with which she has described it, so too she begins by attributing certain qualities to a man and ends up seduced by a creature of her own imagination. Fanni Butlerd well knows that if her lover has become more handsome, it is only because she perceives him as such, and if he is able to charm her, it is because she confers on him the ability to do so. Even thoroughly in love, Fanni has the necessary understanding and frankness to observe to the man she worships that his beauty is in the eye of the beholder: "C'est mon amour qui t'embellit, il te donne des grâces avec lesquelles tu me séduis... Mon Dieu, quand je ne t'aimais point, tu n'étais pas plus beau qu'un autre au moins" (LXXXI). [2] After the affair is ended, moreover, Alfred inevitably returns to the state of an ordinary mortal; Fanni comments, "cette idole chérie, adorée, dénuée des ornements dont mon imagination l'avait embellie, ne m'offre plus qu'une esquisse imparfaite" (CXVI). What is singular about these heroines is not just that their vision is clouded by love, but that they perceive that to be so.

---

[1] In a 1771 letter to Robert Liston, Mme Riccoboni calls him "l'idole que mon imagination a consacrée" (N. 75). See also letter 104 in *Les Liaisons dangereuses*, where Mme de Merteuil speaks of women who are passionately in love: "Leur tête exaltée ne rêve qu'agréments et vertus; elles en parent à plaisir celui qu'elles préfèrent," until finally, "dupes de leur propre ouvrage, elles se prosternent pour l'adorer" (p. 242).

[2] There is a comparison to be made here between Fanni Butlerd and her model, Crébillon's Marquise, who is also sensitive to these properties of love, but sees love as *reflected* in herself rather than finding its source of energy there. While Fanni notices a change in her perception of Alfred, the Marquise notices a difference in her *own* person: "C'est mon amour pour vous qui m'embellit," she remarks. (*Lettres de la marquise de M*** au comte de R****, p. 128.)

Even if the heroine voluntarily blinds herself in favor of the lover, that is, even if the illusion is of her own making, love is nonetheless an illusion. In the final analysis, this most glorious of experiences seldom yields what it seemed to promise; almost invariably, it develops that the changes wrought by love were illusory. Love is a sort of powerful charm, an enchanted state of colors, feelings and lights, but it is not the real world, and it must eventually come to an end. Juliette Catesby describes the experience as a "voile aimable" which is finally lifted (VI). The awakening from this state can be brutal, as in the case of Mme de Raisel: "Ce qui avait fait le charme de sa vie se peignit à ses yeux comme une illusion fantastique, comme un songe dont le réveil dissipait l'agréable erreur" (*Histoire du Marquis de Cressy*, p. 117).

Even at love's end, the Riccoboni heroine's discernment does not desert her. When the illusion of love has been dissipated, she is able to judge the experience accurately, clear-headedly and without self-indulgence. When Alfred is about to wed someone else, yet begs Fanni to continue loving him, she justly observes that what he misses is not her affection but its transforming glance: "Vous ne regrettez pas ma tendresse, mais cette admiration dont vous avez si longtemps joui; elle vous flattait. Ma prévention avait élevé un temple à vos vertus; vous voyez tomber le voile de l'illusion; vous vous efforcez de le rattacher sur mes yeux" (CVIII). The male figures themselves can sometimes perceive the role which self-delusion may play in their mistress: to an unreceptive Juliette Catesby, her repentant lover cries "Ah, remettez sur vos yeux le bandeau de l'amour! qu'il vous cache mes fautes" (XXXV).

The end of the illusion is all the more painful because love is so utterly essential to the woman. Such is her need to love that the particular object is secondary in importance to the existence of the phenomenon. Adélaïde's love for the unworthy Cressy is so great that it detaches itself from its object: "sa passion devint si puissante sur son âme, que l'ingratitude et la perfidie du marquis ne purent dans la suite ni l'éteindre ni la lui rendre moins chère" (*Histoire du Marquis de Cressy*, p. 7). Like Fanni Butlerd, who takes nearly two months to break up with Alfred after discovering that he plans to marry another woman, Adélaïde is so overwhelmingly disposed in Cressy's favor that she cannot force herself to abjure him without the utmost difficulty. When finally she has no other choice than to do so, it is less her former lover than the experience of loving which leaves an aching void:

> Ce n'est pas toujours son amant qu'on regrette le plus, quand on est forcée de lui retirer son cœur, c'est le sentiment dont on était touchée, c'est le prestige aimable qui s'évanouit, c'est le plaisir d'aimer; plaisir si grand pour une âme tendre, qu'elle ne voit rien qui puisse remplacer la douce habitude qu'elle avait prise de s'y livrer. (P. 58)

When love is finished, there is nothing capable of replacing it: only sadness, languor and emptiness lie ahead.

For the Riccoboni heroine is solipsistic: everything from start to finish takes place within herself. She may walk a parallel path with a man but, as we have said, there is no real communion; even in those cases where the overall tone is relatively positive, there is little sense of a *shared* experience. The role of the letter is central in this kind of system; for dealing with the lover by letter masks the fact that no authentic communication may be taking place. Where no real interaction is possible, the woman may at least relate to paper. It is interesting in this context that the letters of the heroine alone appear: she may indicate — as does Fanni Butlerd — that her lover does respond, but his apparent silence, insofar as the real reader is concerned, may be interpreted symbolically.

Although the Riccoboni heroine has an enormous need to love, she seldom believes for very long that love will work out: she may at moments abandon herself to enthusiasm and elation, but at heart she has the tragic sense that the whole thing may well be doomed. This contradiction between her desire to love and her innate and sometimes unconscious distrust of love inevitably creates tension: love in opposition to fear, involvement as against a defensive, stonelike indifference.

Fanni Butlerd is the most striking example: immensely enthusiastic about love, she nevertheless finds her very capacity for passion frightening and excessive: "Il faut modérer cette passion, en ralentir les mouvements, les rendre plus supportables; le tiers de mon amour serait assez" (LXXXIX). But precisely because she cannot diminish her love, Fanni's posture is uncomfortable; she must go on loving Alfred, but is always prey to anxiety, and alludes repeatedly to the possibility that he may eventually desert her. "Si vous cessiez de m'aimer, si je vous perdais" (XXVII), she cries out; and again: "Cet empire que vous avez sur moi, qui vous flatte à présent, qui vous paraît si doux, ne vous lassera-t-il pas un jour?" (XXXII). So great is Fanni's obsession with this vision of Alfred's desertion, that she herself, consciously or no, probably hastens the dénouement by dwelling on it. This premonition is apparent from a remark like the following, which Fanni makes at the height of the affair, when everything seems to be going smoothly: "Je suis comme un vaporeux qui, jouissant d'une santé parfaite, à force de s'en occuper, envisage à chaque instant tous les maux qui peuvent la détruire, et voit la mort, sans que rien lui en découvre les approches" (XCVI). The comparison also serves to illustrate the psychological richness of Fanni's character; the ambivalence of her stance is striking. From the outset she manifests, along with her willingness to love, a deep-seated fear. In one of her earliest letters, she tells Alfred, "Je vous aime, mais je crains les suites d'une passion dont je sens que je ferais ma seule affaire" (VI).

Obviously, Fanni is acutely aware of her own proclivity for total commitment, and dubious about Alfred's capacity for fidelity; but her hesitations seem to go even deeper than this. She is subject to an undefined revulsion which distresses her because she cannot understand it. Fanni is fascinated by the idea of physical love at the same time that she is terrorized by it: "Je sens qu'il m'est difficile de résister longtemps à la douce espérance de vous rendre heureux, j'éloigne les occasions, n'est-ce pas avouer que je les crains? Mais d'où vient que je suis révoltée à la seule idée?" (XIII). Shortly thereafter she again evokes this mysterious dread — this horror of the flesh — which she shares to a greater or lesser degree with most of the other Riccoboni heroines; she speaks of "tant de préjugés à vaincre, une si longue habitude de penser que rien ne pouvait les détruire; je ne sais quel effroi" as the main obstacles to love. *Préjugé* is one of the words which Fanni uses often in attempting to explain her hesitations; she wishes this *préjugé* did not exist, but at times feels powerless to combat it. It seems clear that Fanni is referring to a personal rather than a social prejudice — to a complex of emotions involving both a profound distrust of physical commitment and a dread of dangerous emotional ties. Laurent Versini compares the resistance of Crébillon's marquise, who alludes to an ambiguous *devoir*, with Fanni's evocation of an equally ill-articulated *préjugé*. In both cases, as with the Princesse de Cléves, he believes that the underlying explanation is fear of love:

> En fait les héroines de tous ces romans, chez Crébillon, chez Mme Riccoboni, déjà chez Mme de Lafayette, résistent au nom d'une sorte de fidélité aux conditions qu'elles ont fixées elles-mêmes, dictées par l'honneur au dix-septième siècle, par l'honnêteté au dix-huitième, plus qu'au nom de la véritable vertu. Et surtout par peur de l'amour. L'amour est un mal, le bonheur qu'il donne est passager. Sans illusions sur la fidelité que leur conserverait leur amant ... ces femmes trahies ou ces jeunes veuves, ont comme l'Hortense du *Prince travesti*, tiré de leur expérience une philosophie désenchantée qui doit encore plus à l'exemple d'une autre, de cette princesse de Clèves dont le modèle est présent en filigrane derrière toutes ces figures de femmes blessées. [3]

An important difference between Fanni and the heroine of Mme de Lafayette is that Fanni's resistance is purely provisional. Any effort to interpret her words, moreover, is complicated by the fact that the arguments which she uses to protest her virtue and to combat the attraction which Alfred holds for her, are part of a conventional rhetoric on the subject which both she and Alfred understand. They both know implicitly that eventually, and in spite of all she says, Fanni will decide to "le rendre heureux."

Adélaïde du Bugei, in *Histoire du Marquis de Cressy*, is a slighty different case. Her fears are just as deep as Fanni's, but she is initially less aware of them; moreover, while she uses the same terminology as Fanni does, she does not grasp the accepted meaning. It is late evening and Cressy, the would-be seducer to whom Adélaïde has admitted her love, has led her into the garden:

---

[3] *Laclos et la tradition*, pp. 111-12.

> sans prévoir où la guidait une question captieuse, elle y avait répondu, elle avait dit qu'elle désirait *qu'il fût heureux*, qu'elle ferait tout pour assurer *son bonheur*: elle le disait encore quand la témérité du Marquis portée à l'extrême, la tirant de cette ivresse dangereuse, lui rendit sa raison, et la force de s'opposer à ses entreprises. (P. 54)

Adélaïde's difficulty results from the fact that, with her extreme youth and inexperience, she is not aware of the connotation which convention has conferred on the terms "être heureux" and "bonheur." When she realizes that her own understanding of these words differs from the Marquis', she becomes conscious of the necessity to defend herself and has no alternative but flight. Whereas Fanni does in fact consent to become Alfred's mistress in spite of her reservations, Adélaïde only briefly seems to do so; Adélaïde's relationship with Cressy essentially ends at this point, and Fanni's and Alfred's moves to a different level.

While Fanni is afraid and hesitant as she takes this step, her strength resides in the fact that there is no concomitant sense of guilt. Because of her force of character, the path of feeling becomes for this heroine the path of virtue. She is concerned about being hurt, but she is not haunted by the spectre of lost innocence. When she gives in to Alfred, she is careful to turn what might have been a moment of defeat into a moment of glory, even going so far as to congratulate herself for not having succumbed in an instant of weakness, but for having bestowed her favors consciously: "Je n'ai point cédé: un moment de délire ne m'a point mise dans ses bras; je me suis donnée; mes faveurs sont le fruit de l'amour, sont le prix de l'amour" (XXXVI). Fanni thereby illustrates the principle that virtue, for the eighteenth-century heroine, has a way of tailoring itself to the occasion: "Avant la chute la vertu consiste à résister à l'amour. Après la chute, elle se transforme en un attachement héroïque à cet amour." [4]

The deep fear of physical and emotional involvement to which these heroines are prey and which exists side by side with a

---

[4] Robert Mauzi, *L'idée du bonheur dans la littérature et la pensée française au 18ᵉ siècle* (Paris, 1960), p. 479.

need to give themselves in love, is often expressed as a preoccupation with the notion of *tranquillité*. The word itself forms a sort of leitmotif throughout the novels of Mme Riccoboni, as it did in Crébillon's *Lettres de la marquise,* as it will in the letters of Laclos' Mme de Tourvel. Heroines in the lineage of the Princesse de Clèves are wary of their own sensibility because it engages them in situations detrimental to their *repos*. They resist passion, therefore, in the name of tranquility, raising continually the question of whether the turmoil of love is preferable to the peace of indifference. Crébillon's marquise frequently protests that if she is not happy without love, she is at least *tranquille;* the following words of the marquise might as well have been spoken by Fanni Butlerd while she is resisting Alfred: "Je ne suis point heureuse, mais je suis tranquille: cette tranquillité m'a trop coûté, je la possède depuis trop peu de temps, enfin j'en connais trop les charmes pour vouloir m'exposer à la perdre." [5] And after committing herself, Fanni is often preoccupied with her lost peace; identifying love with agitation, she looks back nostalgically to her former existence, "tranquille," "paisible," and "indifférente," when she was still as impressionless, she says, as marble:

> Avant que vous me fissiez éprouver ces mouvements auxquels vous voulez que mon âme s'abandonne, j'étais tranquille, contente.... Semblable à Pygmalion, vous animez un marbre; craignez qu'il ne vous reproche un jour de l'avoir tiré de sa paisible indifférence. (VII)

Later, tormented by Alfred's demands, she cries out, "O ma paisible indifférence, qu'êtes-vous devenue?" (XXXIV). This dialectic between the tumult of love and the tranquility of unconcern is continued in the later novels. Sophie de Vallière, for example, is aware of a change in her perception of time when she falls in love, but she indicates that this change is not necessarily for the better. She nostalgically recalls the period of her life when time flowed smoothly and painlessly by, when "toutes les heures passaient sans être marquées par des craintes, par d'im-

---

[5] *Lettres de la marquise de M*** au comte de R***,* p. 20.

puissants désirs, par de sombres réflexions ou de tristes regrets" (XXXIV).

The corollary of this nostalgia for lost peace which affects Fanni and the others is that, when the love affair is over, they can comfort themselves with the recovery of their tranquility. There is, no doubt, a certain amount of bad faith involved when they assure themselves that, after all (and now that it is too late to change anything), they are better off without love. But there is also honest relief: "On est bien tranquille, quand on n'envisage point de pertes égales à celles qu'on a faites" (*Lettres de Fanni Butlerd*, CIV). [6]

In the system which they have erected and which has love for its center, the only alternative to being in love is, in fact, total unconcern. Unlike Rousseau's Julie, who finds satisfaction in raising her children and looking after her household and workers, unlike the sensitive souls in the novels of Baculard d'Arnaud, who delight in ministering to those less fortunate than themselves, the heroines of Mme Riccoboni give little thought to altruism as a possible way of life. If love does not work out for them, there is nothing left but to abandon the world. Two other young Riccoboni heroines to whom love is not kind decide, like Fanni and the Princesse de Clèves, to finish out their lives in retreat. They are Adélaïde du Bugei and the heroine of *Histoire de Miss Jenny*. Adélaïde retires to a convent not as is traditionally the case merely to seek consolation, but also to preclude the possibility of falling in love again and being hurt once more. When Adélaïde receives a visit in retreat from the woman for whom Cressy betrayed her (and who married him only to be betrayed in turn), she congratulates herself on having escaped from a world where happiness is of such short duration:

> la charmante recluse se consola de n'avoir point joui du bonheur qu'un instant pouvait changer en amertume; elle plaignit celle dont elle enviait peut-être auparavant la

---

[6] After she realizes that she has been permanently abandoned, the Portuguese nun too recalls her former tranquility, but her stance is different from Fanni's: to her lover she writes, "je vous remercie dans le fond de mon cœur du désespoir que vous me causez, et je déteste la tranquilité où j'ai vécu avant que je vous connusse" (*Lettres portugaises*, p. 50).

> félicité; et pour toujours à l'abri des cruelles peines qui déchiraient le cœur de la Marquise, elle s'applaudit du choix qu'elle avait fait. (P. 115)

If there is no joy outside of love, Adélaïde self-complacently observes, at least there is no real misery either. Similarly, when the fiancé of Miss Jenny is killed in a duel, she retires from society and in her seclusion finds great solace in the knowledge that the turbulence which has characterized her young life is at an end:

> Je suis encore bien triste, il est vrai, mais je suis moins agitée; je pleure souvent, mais à présent mes larmes coulent sans effort, elles soulagent mon cœur. Je n'envisage point un avenir heureux, mais j'entrevois dans l'éloignement une vie tranquille. (Part IV, p. 118)

Jenny, Adélaïde and Fanni consider their emotional lives as spent after one brief but painful encounter with passion; their hurt is so insurmountable that they assume a basically defensive posture, valuing their prophylactic attitude more highly than the possibility of happiness with its accompanying risks. In this sense there is a difference to be noted between their case and that of the Princesse de Clèves, whose renunciation is based not on hurt but on fear; the Riccoboni heroines, in spite of their fear, do give passion a chance — but only a single chance.

Compelled to choose between exposure to pain and indifference, Jenny and Adélaïde opt for the latter. But at least one Riccoboni protagonist seems to have discovered a better solution. Mme de Monglas, an episodic character in *Lettres de Sophie de Vallière*, is married to an elderly and benevolent man. This young woman was originally destined by her family for the convent, as was customary in order to preserve the inheritance of an older brother; but M. de Monglas agreed to marry her without a dowry. Since he requires of her only filial devotion, the young wife is quite happy to escape the necessity of physical love. She considers herself particularly fortunate, moreover, to have found constancy and to be spared the upset which usually accompanies emotional and epidermal involvement. Of Sophie and her fiancé, who are in love and about to be wed, Mme de

Monglas remarks, "En considérant ces deux amants, que l'on nomme ici *amants heureux,* je m'assure avec bien du plaisir, que la douce paix de mon âme est préférable à un sentiment dont les délices si vantés peuvent produire les mêmes effets que la douleur" (XLIV). Whether the agitation of love constitutes delight or grief, she deems herself lucky to be free of it.

* * *

It is natural that, in a system where love is so fearful, a premium should be placed on an affective relationship like the one just described — where there is less likelihood of deception and betrayal, where there is real communion, and which is compatible with tranquility. Friendship between two persons of the same sex also meets these qualifications. While love is the primary concern in these novels, it cannot be understood except in light of the meaning of friendship, for the two relationships are continually compared and contrasted. Built on a firmer basis than love, which is so frequently unreliable, friendship is in many ways a superior sentiment: "Différente de l'amour, l'amitié ne se nourrit pas des erreurs de l'imagination"; it is "douce, égale, paisible" (*Lettres de Mylord Rivers,* X). Juliette Catesby says she prefers it to love because it is more rational and less easily shattered; she describes love as a "sentiment moins volontaire et plus tumultueux," whereas of it she declares that "les qualités qui l'ont fait naître ne doivent rien à l'illusion: le temps ni l'éloignement ne pourront jamais le détruire" (VI). Love, based on illusion, is an ephemeral and risky business; the friend, on the other hand, is someone whose worth is real and not imagined, and in him reside constancy and security. Most of these heroines possess a true friend; in *Lettres de Juliette Catesby* and *Lettres de Sophie de Vallière,* we know little more about the friend than that she incarnates undying devotion and constant willingness to listen and comfort. Hortense, in *Histoire du Marquis de Cressy,* is one of the rare persons in these works to betray a friend. Living at the expense of the generous Mme de Raisel, Hortense sets out to seduce the husband of her protectress; apropos of the priorities which Hortense establishes, the narrator exclaims, "Quelle différence, quelle perte! quoi qu'on puisse penser dans l'égarement de son cœur, un amant ne vaut pas une amie" (pp. 98-99).

The dialogue between passion and apathy, between the agitation of love and the peace of friendship, is never completely resolved in these novels; the continuing debate between opposing forces and desires constitutes their richness. While Juliette Catesby may at one time declare that love is the only emotion which a woman should ever allow herself to experience, Fanni Butlerd sighs in response, "Mais il faut une passion comme la mienne pour juger de ce qu'on perdrait à ne pas aimer" (LXXXIV). No resolution of the problem seems possible, yet we might say in conclusion that the ideal situation — if it could be prolonged indefinitely — may well be one in which the woman has both a lover and a friend in whom to confide her love. The notion of confiding is of course closely related to that of friendship.[7] Moreover, this conception of friendship as necessitating the communication of one's trials and pleasures brings us back to the very form with which we are dealing: it is the underlying principle of most of Mme Riccoboni's epistolary novels, where a heroine writes not only to keep her friend abreast of her joys and woes, but also because she feels the need of pouring out her heart to someone in whose affections she can be secure. Significantly, Fanni Butlerd, who corresponds with her lover rather than with a confidante, imposes on him the functions of a friend. She insists on his dual role and tends to see in him two distinct persons, with two different responsibilities toward her: "Félicitez-moi, mon cher amant, j'ai un ami que rien n'égale; et vous, mon tendre ami, partagez ma joie, j'ai un amant adorable. A quel être bienfaisant

---

[7] "L'amour ne dispense pas de l'amitié. Le bonheur consiste à éprouver simultanément les deux sentiments.... [L'amitié] a sa place comme accompagnement et commentaire de l'amour; l'ami est cet être précieux auquel on parle de ce qu'on aime" (Robert Mauzi, *L'idée du bonheur*, p. 472). The hero of Prévost's *Cleveland* (1731) writes, "Tu me rends heureux, ma chère amie; mais pour sentir tout le bonheur que je goûte avec toi, il faut que j'aye quelqu'un qui ne soit pas toi, non seulement à qui je puisse le dire, mais en qui j'aye assez de confiance pour le dire avec goût, et qui m'aime assez pour trouver du plaisir à l'entendre" (*Le Philosophe anglais* [*Cleveland*], in *Œuvres choisies de Prévost* [Paris: Leblanc, 1810], V, p. 283).

m'adresserai-je pour le prier de me les conserver tous deux?" (XXIX).

* * *

The Independent Woman

Many a novel had of course been based on the notion that love is an ongoing struggle; Agathe in Baculard d'Arnaud's *Les Epoux malheureux* (1745), for example, observes that passion is always subject to adversity: "Eh! peut-on aimer tranquillement? montre-moi un amour, une passion telle que la nôtre, qui n'ait pas été soumise à des traverses." [8] But while every love story is an account of the obstacles by which lovers are beset, the novels of Mme Riccoboni are distinct in the nature of the obstacles encountered: here they are not exterior to the lovers, but are to be found within them. Frequently in the novel of this period, the chief deterrent to a love relationship is parental or social pressure, striving to hinder a match which would be considered ill-assorted. *Les Illustres Françaises*, *Mémoires du Comte de Comminge* and *Les Epoux malheureux* are all typical in this regard. In the last case, M. de la Bédoyère and Agathe Sticotti must face repeated trials and persecutions because it is not considered proper for well-bred young men to marry actresses. In the novels of Mme Riccoboni, on the other hand, difficulties arise less frequently from social or familial opposition than as the result of the inherent nature of men and women: the lovers do not face common trials together, but are pitted one against the other.

Parental pressure is minimal because parents are virtually nonexistent. This is an interesting characteristic in view of Mme Riccoboni's family history: Christophe de Heurles left Marie-Jeanne and her mother shortly after his daughter's birth; the novelist never really knew her father, and with her embittered mother her relationship always remained unhappy. Besides, Mme Riccoboni herself had no children. The novels which she wrote seem to reflect this background: none of the principal heroines

---

[8] *Les Epoux malheureux* (Paris: Laporte, 1783) I, 136.

she created ever conceives a child, and in only three cases do their parents figure at all in the action: in *Histoire du Marquis de Cressy, Lettres de Sophie de Vallière* and *Histoire de Miss Jenny*. In the first of these, Adélaïde du Bugei has a father, but he is one of the least important factors in his daughter's drama. In the first place, he does nothing to counter her fatal penchant for Cressy (on the contrary, he tries to persuade the faithless Cressy to marry her, but fails); and, after her heartbreak, he is powerless to prevent her from retiring to a convent. In both *Histoire de Miss Jenny* and *Lettres de Sophie de Vallière*, a good deal of the novel is devoted to the story of the heroine's parents; but all four parents involved are nonetheless dead by the time the girls are a few days old and, moreover, while they lived their conduct was almost uniformly reprehensible: Jenny was born out of wedlock, while a breach of friendship on the part of Sophie's misguided parents resulted in their deaths, Sophie's desolation, and the despair of their friend Lindsey. In *Lettres de Sophie de Vallière*, though, one mother does appear: this is the mother of the Marquis de Germeuil, whom Sophie loves; but she, like the father of Adélaïde, is a weak element in the plot. Although she would clearly oppose having the penniless Sophie as a daughter-in-law, she is not given the opportunity to disapprove because Sophie refuses to hear Germeuil's suit until her fortune is established. Miss Jenny does have a wicked grandfather, but it is his very refusal to recognize her which leaves her open to misfortune. He has no positive effect on the outcome of events; most significant is the fact that when, at the story's end, he attempts to reassert his authority over her, she repudiates him and retires from society. When parents do appear, then, they are minor factors; and in most of the novels, they do not figure at all in the central action.

Husbands are as little in evidence as parents; it is noteworthy that not one of the Riccoboni heroines is married to begin with, and that the novels generally end either at the point where the heroine is on the brink of wedlock (*Lettres de Juliette Catesby, Histoire d'Ernestine, Lettres de Madame de Sancerre, Lettres de Sophie de Vallière* and *Lettres de Mylord Rivers*) or at the point where marriage has been rendered impossible (*Lettres de Fanni Butlerd* and *Histoire de Miss Jenny*).

Most of the female characters in these novels are either orphans or widows — both of which are, of course, rather conventional figures in the eighteenth-century novel — and therefore the norms by which they live are largely of their own making. Subject to no immediate outside authority, their guides are instinct and conscience. Among the orphans in the novels of Mme Riccoboni are the female protagonists not only of *Histoire de Miss Jenny* and *Lettres de Sophie de Vallière*, but also of *Histoire d'Ernestine* and *Lettres de Mylord Rivers*. The origins of the first three are either mysterious or disputed: Sophie is a foundling, Jenny the illegitimate offspring of noble parents whose families refuse to recognize her, and Ernestine a young German immigrant to France whose parentage and ancestry, though obscure, are certainly undistinguished. Thus they are totally removed from familial influence. They are obliged to fend for themselves early in life, but they enjoy the freedom to make their own decisions and are spared meddling which might tend to thwart their love lives or coerce them into unpalatable marriages.

There is an even more impressive proliferation of widows than of orphans, and while in these instances the first husband was chosen by the family, the women are free as the novel opens to choose the second — if, indeed, they determine that there is to be a second. They include one of the protagonists of *Histoire du Marquis de Cressy;* twenty-six year old Mme de Raisel is reminiscent of the beautiful and *sensible* Mme de Selve in Duclos' *Confessions du Comte de* *** (1741). Like her, Mme de Raisel was sacrificed by her family to an unattractive and elderly husband and, finally free of him, is not initially inclined ever to remarry: "La comtesse, veuve depuis deux ans d'un mari qu'elle n'aimait pas, dont l'âge avancé et l'humeur fâcheuse ne lui avaient fait connaître le mariage que par ses dégoûts, semblait s'être destinée à vivre libre" (p. 4). But while Mme de Selve is still too young to give her own hand in marriage, Mme de Raisel is now free to determine her fate. Financially and socially independent, she need consult only her personal inclinations in the matter; so when she selects the despicable Marquis de Cressy as a mate, the error is of her own making.

In *Histoire de Miss Jenny*, one of the protagonists is the heroine's friend, Mylady d'Anglesey, a twenty-one year old widow, while in *Lettres de Mylord Rivers,* one of the chief correspondents, Lady Orrery, is also a widow. Juliette Catesby ("mariée à seize ans, veuve à dix-huit") survives a jealous old husband, and in this same novel, widows appear in several episodic roles as well; the heroine describes, for example, a visit to a delightful home:

> la gaîté y préside depuis deux mois: elle appartient à une veuve qui n'a pas encore vingt ans. Enchantée de son nouvel état, elle vient ici passer l'année de son deuil, seulement pour méditer en repos sur le choix qu'elle fera, lorsque la bienséance lui permettra de remplacer un vieux mari, qu'elle haïssait de tout son cœur. (V)

Freedom of choice regarding a second husband is, for all these women, a cherished privilege of widowhood, and the one to which they most constantly allude in describing their situation.

Lettres de Madame de Sancerre is the novel in which widows are most in evidence and here the autonomy they so highly prize becomes a leitmotif. Mme de Sancerre herself is a young woman of twenty-six who was married at sixteen and widowed at twenty-two [9]; her two closest friends are Mme de Mirande and Mme de Martigues, also young widows of a few years, and the plot revolves around the theme of widowhood which links the destinies of the three. The connection is established early on by the Comte de Piennes, suitor of Mme de Martigues: "Si une de ces trois charmantes veuves, dit-il, rentrait sous le joug, les deux autres suivraient son exemple" (II). Piennes' use of the word "joug" is significant because it is in precisely this light that our three young heroines tend to view wedlock. Husbands are seen as arbitrary and unreasonable masters; Mme de Martigues, the most vociferous of the group, insists on the loss of liberty which the institution entails:

> l'idée d'un mari me ferait fuir au bout de l'univers. C'est une créature si familière, si exigeante, si impérieuse. Comment me résoudre à donner à un homme le droit

---

[9] According to F. C. Green, "Mme de Sancerres [sic] is the first interesting widow in French fiction, because she is neither funny nor immoral" (*French Novelists, Manners and Ideas* [London: Dent and Sons, 1928], p. 182).

d'entrer chez moi comme chez lui? De rester là, de me gêner, de m'ennuyer, de me contrarier, de prétendre, de vouloir, enfin de m'imposer des lois? (XLI)

In a more flippant tone, she comments on the unpleasant nature of most men and on the perversity of her fate in sending her a pretender as persistent as Piennes when the majority of males are so notoriously inconstant: "il s'obstine à *m'aimer,* à *m'adorer,* à vouloir être *mon mari.* Voyez si mon sort n'est pas fâcheux, bizarre. Peut-être n'est-il dans le monde qu'un seul homme constant: j'ai eu le malheur de le rencontrer" (XLI). All of these women are circumspect about romance and marriage, and jealous of their right to turn down anyone of whom their heart does not entirely approve. Even one of their married friends supports them in their aversion for marriage: Mme de Thémines considers herself happily married, yet she declares, "je ne saurais désapprouver une femme libre en la voyant éviter un joug pesant. Le meilleur mari est... est un mari" (XLI). There is an interesting similarity between her attitude and that of so many of Marivaux's theatrical heroines, who are fond of their liberty and wary of allowing a swain to become a husband. In *Le Jeu de l'Amour et du Hasard,* Silvia delivers a lengthy speech about the risks of wedlock, which she closes with the remark, "Songe à ce que c'est qu'un mari." Her servant's humorous retort sets off her attitude even more strikingly: "Un mari? c'est un mari; vous ne deviez pas finir par ce mot-là; il me raccommode avec tout le reste" (act I, scene 1). All three widows in *Lettres de Madame de Sancerre* eventually decide, like Silvia, to take the chance and wed — though the Marivaux character does so only after putting her prospective husband to trials of which the less wily heroines of Mme Riccoboni would never dream.

It is against this background of freedom from family constraints that the drama of Mme Riccoboni's heroines is played out, and the predominance of widows and orphans in the eight novels is not accidental. It is an important consideration in understanding their plight, for the tragedies or near-tragedies which so often afflict them are rarely the result of outside interference. All these young widows and orphans are at liberty to give their hearts and hands when and where they choose, and this makes all the more impressive one of the aforementioned themes of the novels, that if women experience sorrow and disappointment in their love affairs, it is for only one reason: the dreadful character of most men. When the woman's heart is broken, when her life is ruined, when she is in some way temporarily or permanently victimized, the responsible party is none other than the man she loves; if love is an uphill struggle it is because it necessarily involves two people, and one of them, morally speaking, is inherently inferior.

* * *

Four love idylls

While the novels paint a somewhat desolate picture of relations between the sexes, four short stories which Mme Riccoboni published in 1779 and 1780 in the *Bibliothèque des Romans* evoke the ideal in this regard. The tales, which were presented as extracts from old manuscripts, are set in a time and place where men and women are equally sincere and generous, and where lovers are worthy and faithful and — in spite of temporary difficulties — attain lasting happiness in the end.[10] When we consider that Mme Riccoboni's earlier works almost all bemoan the pitfalls of love and evoke the impasse to which the sensitive woman is brought by cruelty and infidelity, it may seem surprising that she should now produce four such idylls as these. But she was becoming old and perhaps tiring of the themes of grief and despair with which she had previously concerned herself.

---

[10] In a letter to Liston, Mme Riccoboni spoke of the vogue of medieval or pseudo-medieval settings and of her own endeavors: "Je fais des histoires anciennes. Cela vous paraît assez ridicule. J'ai pourtant fort bien réussi à peindre la naïveté du siècle de Louis Onze. Je viens de remonter à celui de Saint-Louis. On donne depuis quatre ans des extraits qui paraissent tous les mois. On cherche tous les vieux romans, on prend ceux de toutes les nations. Cet ouvrage plaît. Ceux qui inventent des historiettes dans ce livre les annoncent comme tirés de très anciens manuscrits et s'amusent des sots qui donnent dans le piège et cherchent de bonne foi à se procurer la lecture des manuscrits. Cette petite occupation me rapporte un profit raisonnable et me distrait" (N. 136).

Moreover, while her earlier personal life had been disappointing, owing to her husband's wretched behavior, her ill-fated romance, and her resentful mother, by this time both mother and husband had died — relieving her of an emotional and financial burden — and the lover who abandoned her was a thing of the distant past. She was a well-known author, she had a number of friends, and she seems not to have been unhappy with her lot. James Nicholls points out Mme Riccoboni's increasing pessimism in her later years, her growing conviction that "there was more evil than good in the world." [11] While Mme Riccoboni did indeed lament the state of the universe and the fate of mankind — war, poverty, disease, death — and while she did view "le genre humain" as cruel and capricious, nevertheless, with her own situation she was well satisfied. To Liston she wrote in 1776, "ma vie est plus heureuse que celle du plus grand potentat de l'univers" (N. 123), and to Garrick the following year, "Que je me trouve heureuse au coin de mon feu, sans préjugés, sans esprit de parti! La paix règne dans mon simple hermitage" (N. 133). In a letter to Philip Thicknesse in 1780, the year of the publication of the short stories, she further expressed her contentment with her situation in these terms:

> J'entends quelquefois des hommes, sur le retour, soupirer, comparer les temps, rappeller des jours qui ne sont plus, se plaindre de ceux dont ils jouissent encore; moi, je ne regrette rien, et mon état présent me paraît le plus doux que le ciel pût m'accorder dans sa bonté. Indépendante, libre, vivant depuis vingt-cinq ans avec une amie dont l'esprit, l'égalité d'humeur, et le caractère aimable répandent un continuel agrément sur notre société, je goûte un tranquille repos.

It is this serenity which is reflected in the short stories.

With her last novel, *Lettres de Mylord Rivers,* Mme Riccoboni had already deviated from the course which she had been following: here the male protagonist is no longer in any sense a villain; he shares almost all the good qualities of the female characters. The four short stories which we will discuss here continue and

---

[11] *Mme Riccoboni's Letters,* introduction.

emphasize this trend. The historical and geographical setting of each is quite exact. *Histoire de Christine, Reine de Suabe* takes place in the eleventh century, "au temps des premières croisades," *Histoire d'Aloïse de Livarot* during the reign of Francis I, *Histoire d'Enguerrand, ou Rencontre dans la forêt des Ardennes* in that of Philip the Bold, and *Histoire des amours de Gertrude* towards the end of the reign of Charles VII. But the use of history in these stories is nonetheless limited. Beyond the mention of a medieval or Renaissance king or event at the beginning of each, the setting of the tales is as vague as is that of the "English" novels: both forms are devoid of realistic detail. Just as we do not know the height of Fanni Butlerd or Juliette Catesby, or the color of their eyes or hair, we learn nothing of how these other heroes and heroines look, dress, or spend their time; we know only that they love. The author uses a conventional remote past to suggest an ideal world of simplicity and sincerity, where all is grace and innocence, where physiognomy is an infallible guide to character and where villains can therefore be recognized at first glance. In this dreamland there occurs an idealization and finalization of love such as the author did not conceive as taking place in her own day. For love, the past is a refuge; in the distant, make-believe traditions of courtly romance Mme Riccoboni finds a possible context for realization of her ideals of pure love, and only here does the ever-present tension of the novels — between the desire to love and the fear of commitment — finally subside.

Christine de Suabe tells the story of a young girl who renounces a throne for the hand of a man of lower rank than herself, while he gives up the prospect of a glorious career as a warrior in order to live an obscure life with her. Christine and Sigefroid escape the court where they were raised and where their roles would have been foreordained, and seek refuge in an enchanted forest where there are no obstacles to their love. There an elderly hermit joins them in matrimony. That their choice was the right one is eminently clear:

> En recevant la foi de l'héritière d'un grand État, Sigefroid renonça, comme elle, à tous les biens que l'association rend précieux, à toutes les apparences du bonheur, et trouva, dans l'abandon de ses biens, souvent plus

enviés que sentis, cette félicité intérieure, pure, durable, dont la source est en nous-mêmes. (P. 110)

Eventually, Christine's father discovers them, but this once callous man has been softened by a life of loneliness; impressed by the bliss which the couple has found, he gives them his blessings and returns each year to visit them and their children. The greatest happiness, he has learned, comes only with loving and being loved.

Aloïse de Livarot concerns a little girl who is all delicacy and sweetness, and a turbulent but good-hearted boy. Affianced at birth, they detest each other on first meeting; when the time comes for them to marry, each remembers his initial unfavorable impressions and determines to avoid the union by running away from home. But the destructive and ebullient little boy has grown into a brave and chivalrous warrior, and the overly fussy girl has become a splendid young woman. They meet on a foreign shore where Olivier has the good fortune to save Aloïse from a would-be abductor, and they fall in love before each discovers the true identity of the other.

The hero of *Histoire d'Enguerrand* is a noble but impoverished young man who does not feel he may aspire to the hand of the girl he loves, who, unbeknownst to him, returns his affections. The wealthy Blanche de Réthel, unfortunately, is rather vain (a defect of education, not of character) and unused to young men who do not pay her court; she therefore misinterprets and resents the reserve of Enguerrand. Her ensuing cool treatment causes him to run away to the Ardennes forest. Soon she repents and, believing him dead, disguises herself as a page and makes a pilgrimage to the forest. In a dark cabin she meets Enguerrand who is dressed as a hermit; hearing his voice, Blanche at first thinks she has awakened his ghost. When the two recognize each other, they are immediately reconciled and live happily ever after. Love, once again, has transcended social barriers.

The spontaneity of Mme Riccoboni's writing is evident in the passage where she describes the misunderstanding between the lovers; the narrator, who at other moments remains unobtrusive, suddenly intervenes to comment on the action, asking the questions which the reader might ask and supplying the answers:

Blanche ne remarquait-elle point les qualités distinguées d'Enguerrand? *Pardonnez-moi.* En était-elle touchée? *Peut-être.* Ne lisait-elle pas dans ses yeux, dans son cœur? Ne lui savait-elle pas gré de sa réserve, de son respect? *Eh! mon Dieu, non.* Par une suite de cette éducation, cause des erreurs et des fautes de l'héritière de Réthel, cette réserve, ce respect lui déplaisaient. (P. 16)

In the short stories, as well as in the novels, Mme Riccoboni evidently felt free from constraint in matters of technique. Just as she sometimes briefly abandoned the single-writer formula in *Lettres de Madame de Sancerre* and *Lettres de Juliette Catesby,* here she occasionally violates the silent narrator principle when she wishes to express something which it will not accomodate.

Histoire de Gertrude, finally, tells of a beautiful maiden who lives secluded in a dark castle under the tutelage of a wicked uncle: "ses voisins le nommèrent Richard le Hautain; et ses vassaux, moins polis, l'appelèrent tout bonnement Richard le Mauvais" (p. 65). Richard is the complete villain and his infamous character is manifest not only in his name but in everything surrounding him; his attendants include "deux écuyers ... l'un boiteux et l'autre louche; six grands vilains hommes d'armes, barbus et mutilés; un Chapelain borgne; un Intendant bègue; une femme de chambre hargneuse et revêche; un concierge bossu" (p. 65). Gertrude escapes from the castle and, disguised as a shepherdess, wins the heart of a nobleman warrior, Roger; he decides to renounce everything and marry Gertrude, whom he takes for a lowly peasant. Only after the ceremony does he discover that she is both noble and wealthy — and independent, too, because Richard has died, leaving her control of her own fortune.

The moral of these short stories is explicit: the ideal life is one of rustic companionship; it includes a simple home, loving children, and quiet but total devotion to one another. The oft-repeated lesson is that the calm of the country rather than the glamor of the court brings real bliss. Happiness is nourished not on change and excitement but on peace and the certainty of being loved: "Aimer, être aimée, ne perdre jamais la présence d'un object chéri, ne point craindre de rivale dans son cœur, voir tous les jours se ressembler, se dire le soir, demain ramènera pour moi les mêmes douceurs, quelle félicité pouvait être plus grande?" (*Christine de Suabe*, p. 74). Passion, on the other hand, destroys. One must never give way to violent feelings; that internal felicity for which one searches remains possible only if "des passions violentes n'arrêtent ni n'épuisent son cours" (*Christine de Suabe*, p. 110). The heroine of the first Riccoboni novel, Fanni Butlerd, had long ago voiced similar aspirations: "Une simple cabane, une âme tendre, un naturel doux, un amant tel que le mien, aimé comme le mien, point de colique, jamais d'absence, que faudrait-il de plus?" (LXXV). But for her the ideal was unattainable; this realization of happiness is relegated to the never-never world of the pastoral, chivalrous knights and damsels in distress.

Despite their clichés, these stories are interesting for a variety of reasons. They are told with Mme Riccoboni's usual verve and delicacy, and their kings, princesses, woodcutters and saintly hermits are in fact rather winsome. Moreover, they provide, as Emily Crosby notes, "des indications de la marche du XVIIIe siècle vers le romantisme." [12] Certain conventional romantic devices are interwoven into all four: they are rife with forced marriages, escapes, disguises, hermits, tombs, epitaphs and the search for solitude. The young women all display an extreme delicacy; for example, they can rarely eat under stress, while their servants, of course, enjoy hearty appetites. The fundamentals of each tale are the same: a brave young man, a beautiful maiden, love and war. The hero generally distinguishes himself brilliantly on the battlefield, rises to great renown and sooner or later wins the hand of the loveliest girl in the land.

One of the ideas which runs through these tales is the notion of nature as a consoling force. Such a theme is altogether absent from the novels, where the heroines are not just insensitive to the attractions of fields and woods, but may even find such things antipathetic. Mme de Sancerre and her friends sustain short periods of country life only by braving it en masse; Juliette Catesby finds everything and everyone outside the capital boring and provincial; and Adeline Rutland unabashedly declares, "Je ne veux ni moutons, ni bergers. Les champs ne me plaisent point,

---

[12] *Une Romancière oubliée*, p. 100.

des amusements rustiques et uniformes sont sans attraits pour moi; le silence des bois m'assoupit, et le murmure des eaux m'endort" (*Lettres de Mylord Rivers,* VI). On the other hand, Christine and Gertrude spend their most blissful moments in the fields, among the sheep, the flowers and the trees.

But there is this in common with the novels: these, too, are essentially love stories, and some of the important aspects under which love is viewed remain the same. In its beginnings it is still confused with friendship by the innocent maiden. Gertrude, like the heroine of *Histoire d'Ernestine,* falls in love without realizing it and, again like Ernestine, must be alerted to her situation by a more experienced girl friend: "Osera-t-elle lever le voile qui cache aux yeux de l'innocente fille, le danger d'une amitié jurée aux bords des ruisseux, sous l'ombre épaisse des bois?" (*Histoire de Gertrude,* p. 115). As in the novels, too, love revolutionizes one's experience of time and place: "une personne aimée semble emporter avec elle tous les agréments du séjour qu'elle quitte ... chaque instant est marqué par le regret d'un moment heureux, et pour une âme tendre tous les jours de l'absence sont des jours perdus" (*Christine de Suabe,* pp. 41-42). Most important, true love is still the desideratum; it alone can make life worth living. But in the short stories the discovery of love always proves felicitous: here love keeps its promises and no longer constitutes, for the woman involved, an unfortunate and unresolvable dilemma. This kind of perfection, however, can exist only in a world of simplicity and innocence. It is not for a society corrupted by civilization, and the author warns her readers of the abyss between their own experience and the idyllic existence achieved by the simple hearts which she portrays: "O vous, enfants d'un siècle éclairé, qui dissertez avec tant d'éloquence sur le bonheur et savez si peu le goûter, ne jugez pas des plaisirs de ces amants sur les vôtres! Pour en apprécier la douceur, il faudrait aimer comme ils aimaient" (*Histoire de Gertrude,* pp. 113-114).[13]

* * *

---

[13] Mme Riccoboni published two more short stories in the *Mercure de France* in 1780 and 1786. The second of them, *Histoire de deux jeunes amies,* is her last work; a complex and romantic tale, better than half of which is a flashback in the form of a letter (itself containing another letter), it has much in common with the novels, but is quite inferior to them.

The predicament of the sensitive woman, artificially resolved in the short stories, constitutes the most poignant element of the main body of Mme Riccoboni's work; she must have attracted many readers, especially female, by her moving and sympathetic portrayal of women and their sufferings. In this respect, the autobiographical nature of the novels should be noted: these are stories *about* women, created by an author who often hides rather ineffectually behind her characters. Her heroines may differ from one work to the next, but they all bear a fundamental resemblance to their creator: they share her sobriety, her passions, her ideals and her priorities. They share, most of all, her disillusionment regarding men: it seems clear that the unhappy married life of Mme Riccoboni, her love affair, and the great value she subsequently attached to friendship — as illustrated by her passionate devotion to Thérèse Biancolelli, to David Garrick and to Robert Liston — counted for a great deal in the invention of her fictional universe. Herself victimized by a jealous mother, an irresponsible husband and an unfaithful lover, Mme Riccoboni tends to view woman as a being with rights and privileges of her own and condemns those elements in society which run counter to female happiness. In her novels, as in those of a successor, Mme de Staël, the destiny of woman is continually probed and her relationship with a masculine world is explored.

The heroines who people these novels are attractive creatures, in many ways and for a variety of reasons. They are, in the first place, by and large realistic, neither all good nor all bad. While they are strongly principled, they have their shortcomings and do occasionally stumble — only bitterly to regret their error. Lady Sara, for example, the mother of the illegitimate heroine of *Histoire de Miss Jenny*, agrees to indulge the impatience of her fiancé just before their wedding, and pays dearly for it when the marriage is called off; and Miss Jenny herself makes a mistake of a different kind, though one which is equally tragic, when she compromises her heart: in an effort to compensate for her want of fortune and position, she twice agrees to marry men she does not love. The first of them fools her with a sham ceremony and the second is slain just before the wedding.

Though similar in many basic ways, these heroines include a number of different types, from the nimble-tongued Juliette and the spunky Adeline to the sweet and retiring Adélaïde du Bugei. In their manner of dealing with society and their response to its dictates, they range from Ernestine, who exclaims, "Ne me dites rien; ne me parlez ni du monde, ni de ses cruelles bienséances; je les rejette si la dureté les accompagne" (p. 112), to Sophie de Vallière, who is quietly resigned to the necessity of sacrificing personal happiness to appearances: "J'aurai sacrifié l'unique agrément de ma vie à la décence, au devoir; il le faut" (XIII). While they are lucid and introspective, they are also impassioned. They emphasize the necessity of virtue, try to balance reason with sentiment, and neglect the role of religion: love is their only god. Fanni Butlerd declares that if ever Alfred stops loving her, she will become a Catholic:

> J'aurai bien du plaisir à me confesser, car je ne parlerai que de mon amant: tous les Saints et toutes les Saintes qui pareront mon Oratoire auront cette aimable physionomie. Le portrait que je tiens de sa main, placé dans le lieu le plus éminent, sera le Patron révéré, le plus révéré dans mon simple Hermitage: couronné de fleurs, et couvert d'un voile léger, il ne sera vu que de moi; il sera toujours le dieu de mon cœur. (LI)

They are at the same time proud and strong, with the requisite moral courage and self-respect to meet their trials and disappointments without flinching; they never revel in their despair. Their pride renders them acutely aware of what they owe to themselves. Because of their strong moral fiber, it is the female characters, seduced and abandoned though they may be, who eventually triumph. Theirs is the knowledge that they have acted in a forthright and courageous manner, and theirs is often the satisfaction of seeing that the men who caused them to suffer are no happier than they. The fate of the Marquis de Cressy is typical: "il fut grand, il fut distingué; il obtint tous les titres, tous les honneurs qu'il avait désirés: il fut riche, il fut élevé: mais il ne fut point heureux" (p. 146). Like Cressy, Danby (the seducer of Miss Jenny) survives to lead a life of misery and remorse in expiation for the evil which he wrought. When Ossery breaks Juliette Catesby's heart by his infidelity, she at least has nothing to reproach herself, while he spends his days pining for his former mistress and lamenting his mistake. The lives of the male characters are often poisoned by their guilt, while the women whom they wronged glory in their moral superiority and their tranquility of mind.

To this extent, then, is Mme Riccoboni a feminist: all the superiority is alloted to the woman, with whose plight the author is in complete sympathy. Mme Riccoboni's feminism, however, is of a personal, non-militant nature; in the matter of woman's rights, she is more tolerant and less demanding than some of her contemporaries. The delicacy of touch which characterizes her manner of writing may also be observed in the context of what she asks. Her novels, unlike Mme de Graffigny's, for example, do not examine woman's education in the home and the convent and point up abuses and possible solutions. Mme de Graffigny is eloquent about the disadvantages of the convent system of education for young women: "on confie le soin d'éclairer leur esprit à des personnes auxquelles on ferait peut-être un crime d'en avoir, et qui sont incapables de leur former le cœur, qu'elles ne connoissent pas." [14] Another of the anti-feminist customs against which Mme de Graffigny inveighs at some length is that of forcing girls into convents in order to avoid cutting the family estate to endow them. Mme Riccoboni touches on these matters only cursorily; they are not her major preoccupations. What she insists on over and again is her belief in women's preeminence and her regret for their suffering at men's hands. She is concerned chiefly with women who are victims of unscrupulous men but who, all the same, are not wholly discontented with their situation because they realize that fulfillment comes only with being loved and that love involves a risk.

Riccoboni heroines do not ask a position of authority or even of equality with men, but are, on the whole, resigned to their subordination. There is nothing revolutionary, for instance, about their conception of the duties of a wife; Miss Jenny envisages woman's position in marriage as naturally and necessarily inferior to that of the man. Just after her bogus marriage to Danby, she learns that he plans to keep her secluded in a country house and

---

[14] *Lettres d'une Péruvienne*, p. 290. In *L'Abeille* and *Suite de l'Abeille*, Mme Riccoboni does criticize contemporary female education.

visit her in the guise of her brother-in-law. Jenny's sensibilities are jolted at the idea of this imposture, but she refrains from complaining: "un instant de réflexion me rappela mes vœux récents, les obligations de mon nouvel état; il ne me convenait plus de m'opposer à la volonté de Sir James" (part II, p. 68). In spite of her repugnance for his bizarre plans, she constantly effaces herself before him: "Je répondis à Sir James que ne séparant plus ses intérêts des miens, je me conformerais à ses volontés, et m'efforcerais de trouver ma félicité dans tout ce qui contribuerait à assurer la sienne" (part II, p. 72). Her revolt occurs only after two years of living in seclusion and posing as Danby's sister-in-law, when she discovers that he has tricked her and she is not in fact married to him. Mme de Sancerre's attitude is similar: married to a spiteful and shameless man with a gift for dissembling, she expends much time and effort attempting to win his love and make their union a success. When she fails, she could still expose his dishonesty, thus ruining him and justifying herself in society's eyes. But she spurns this course of action; instead she retires to her country estate and acquires the reputation of a capricious woman who cares nothing for her devoted husband. Both of these women have what Joachim Merlant calls "l'héroïsme du silence" [15]; they accept their trials and choose rather to suffer than to revolt.

Mme Riccoboni does not demand an upheaval of the social system; she asks only that men, individually and collectively, behave more decently toward women and that the Danbys and Alfreds of the world end their exploitation of the weaker sex. As the Guizots remarked towards the close of the last century, "Ce n'est pas ce qu'on impose aux femmes qui déplaise aux héroines de Mme Riccoboni, mais ce dont on dispense les hommes. C'est moins de leur condition qu'elles se plaignent que des inconvénients qu'elles prétendent qu'on y ajoute." [16] Like Mme de Staël, Mme Riccoboni is interested in women less on a social than on a personal level. The changes which she asks on their behalf are modest, as Joachim Merlant explains:

---

[15] *Le Roman personnel de Rousseau à Fromentin*, p. 6.
[16] M. et Mme Guizot, *Le Temps passé* (Paris: Perrin, 1887), II, 198.

> elle croit que les femmes n'auraient rien à gagner à rivaliser avec les hommes.... Mais elle sent, comme Mme de Staël, que l'homme s'irrite de rencontrer un caractère chez la femme, qu'il s'étonne si elle réclame devant lui des droits d'une personne.... elle demande qu'on reconnaisse une même morale, une même dignité pour les deux sexes, elle exige une estime égale et mutuelle, une honnêteté franche et de bon aloi qui épargne aux uns les manèges hypocrites, qui rende aux autres la pleine disposition de leur sort.[17]

It is because Riccoboni heroines are indeed women of character that they come so violently into conflict with men. But, on the whole, they are resigned to the unfortunate implications of having a sensitive soul; they recognize that it is in the make-up of man to cheat and of woman to forgive. They ask only that the suffering required of them might be a little less terrible.

Although disabused about life, Mme Riccoboni is essentially optimistic: "Ne vaudrait-il pas mieux élever l'âme que de l'abattre?" asks Juliette Catesby (XV). Her tone is discouraged but not usually embittered. In her works there is none of the description of profligacy, none of the cynicism or brutality of tone which characterize the works of some of her contemporaries. She offers instead, in the words of Mme de Staël, "des principes délicats sur la conduite des femmes" [18]; she insists on the beauties of the feminine soul and the uplifting quality of feminine love, and the interest of her work resides largely in the admirable portrayal of the sensitive woman, her joys, her trials and her aspirations.

---

[17] *Le Roman personnel de Rousseau à Fromentin*, pp. 5-6.
[18] *Essai sur les femmes*, in *Œuvres* (Paris: Lefèvre, 1838), I, 145.

A SELECTED BIBLIOGRAPHY

Abensour, Léon. *La Femme et le féminisme avant la Révolution.* Paris: Leroux, 1923.

Anderson, David L. "Abélard and Héloïse: eighteenth-century motif." *Studies on Voltaire and the Eighteenth Century,* LXXXIV (1971).

Ascoli, Georges. "Essai sur l'histoire des idées féministes en France du XVIe siècle à la Révolution." *Revue de Synthèse historique,* XIII (1906), 25-57, 99-106, 161-184.

Baldensperger, Fernand. "Le Genre troubadour." *Études d'Histoire littéraire.* Paris: Hachette, 1907.

Black, Frank Gees. *The Epistolary Novel in the Late Eighteenth Century.* Eugene, Oregon, 1940.

Boutet de Monvel. *L'Amant bourru.* Paris: Duchesne, 1777.

Brooke, Frances. *History of Lady Julia Mandeville.* 2 vols. 3rd edition. Dublin: J. Potts, 1767.

Campardon, Emile. *Les Comédiens du roi de la troupe italienne.* 2 vols. Paris: Berger-Levrault, 1880.

Coulet, Henri. *Le Roman jusqu'à la Révolution.* Vol. I. Paris: Armand Colin, 1967.

Courville, Xavier de. *Luigi Riccoboni dit Lélio.* 2 vols. Paris: Droz, 1945.

Crosby, Emily. *Une Romancière oubliée.* Paris, 1924.

Doudan, X. *Mélanges et Lettres.* Paris: Calmann Lévy, 1876.

Etienne, Servais. *Le Genre romanesque en France.* Paris, 1922.

Fleury, Jean. *Marivaux et le marivaudage.* Paris: E. Plon, 1881.

Foster, James R. *History of the Preromantic Novel in England.* New York: MLA, 1949.

Genlis, Stéphanie Félicité Ducrest de Saint-Aubin, comtesse de. *De l'Influence des femmes sur la Littérature française.* Paris, 1811.

Green, Frederick Charles. *French Novelists, Manners and Ideas.* London: Dent and Sons, 1928.

———. "Robert Liston et Mme Riccoboni." *Revue de Littérature comparée,* 38 (1964), 550-58.

Jost, François. *Essais de littérature comparée.* Vol. II: *Europeana,* Urbana: University of Illinois Press, 1968.

Kavanagh, Julia. *French Women of Letters*. Leipsig: Bernhard Tauchnitz, 1862.

Laporte, Joseph de. *Histoire littéraire des femmes françaises, ou Lettres historiques et critiques*. 5 vols. Paris: Lacombe, 1769.

Mme M. "Mme Riccoboni." *Revue de Paris*, 35 (1841), 184-208.

MacCarthy, B. G. *The Female Pen*. 2 vols. Oxford: Cork University Press, 1946-47.

Marivaux. *La Vie de Marianne*. Ed. Frédéric Deloffre. Paris: Garnier, 1963.

May, Georges. *Le Dilemme du roman au XVIIIe siècle*. New Haven: Yale University Press, 1963.

Merlant, Joachim. *Le Roman personnel de Rousseau à Fromentin*. Paris: Hachette, 1905.

Monglond, André. *Le Préromantisme français*. 2 vols. Grenoble, 1930.

Mooij, A. L. A. *Caractères principaux et tendances des romans psychologiques chez quelques femmes-auteurs, de Mme Riccoboni à Mme de Souza*. Groningen, 1949.

Mornet, Daniel. "Les Enseignements des bibliothèques privées (1750-1780)." *Revue d'Histoire littéraire de la France*, 17 (1910) 449-96.

Mylne, Vivienne. *The Eighteenth-Century French Novel: Techniques of Illusion*. Manchester: Manchester University Press, 1965.

Nicholls, James C. "A Critical Edition of the Correspondence of Mme Riccoboni." Ph.D. Dissertation, University of Wisconsin, 1962.

―――. "Mme Riccoboni in North Carolina." *Revue de Littérature comparée*, 41 (1967), 285-88.

―――. *Mme Riccoboni's Letters to David Hume, David Garrick and Sir Robert Liston: 1764-1783*. Forthcoming.

Price, L. M. "Charlotte Buff, Madame Riccoboni and Sophie Laroche." *The Germanic Review*, VI (January 1931), 1-7.

Riccoboni, Marie-Jeanne Laboras de Mézières. *Œuvres*. 9 vols. Paris: Humblot, 1781.

Rosbottom, Ronald C. "Parody and Truth in Mme Riccoboni's Continuation of La Vie de Marianne." *Studies on Voltaire and the Eighteenth Century*, LXXXI (1971).

Rousset, Jean. "Une forme littéraire: le roman par lettres." *Forme et Signification*. Paris: José Corti, 1962.

Staël, Anne Louise Germaine Necker de. *Œuvres*. 3 vols. Paris: Lefèvre, 1838.

Stewart, Philip. *Imitation and Illusion in the French Memoir-Novel, 1700-1750*. New Haven: Yale University Press, 1969.

Van Tieghem, Paul. "Le roman sentimental en Europe de Richardson à Rousseau." *Revue de Littérature comparée*, 20 (1940), 129-51.

Versini, Laurent. *Laclos et la Tradition*. Paris: Klincksieck, 1968.

Watt, Ian. *The Rise of the Novel: Studies in Defoe, Richardson and Fielding*. Berkeley, 1957.

NORTH CAROLINA STUDIES IN THE ROMANCE LANGUAGES AND LITERATURES

I.S.B.N. Prefix 0-88438

Recent Titles

A CRITICAL EDITION WITH INTRODUCTION AND NOTES OF GIL VICENTE'S "FLORESTA DE ENGAÑOS", by Constantine Christopher Stathatos. 1972. (No. 125). -925-1.

LI ROMANS DE WITASSE LE MOINE. *Roman du treizième siècle.* Édité d'après le manuscrit, fonds français 1553, de la Bibliothèque Nationale, Paris, par Denis Joseph Conlon. 1972. (No. 126). -926-X.

EL CRONISTA PEDRO DE ESCAVIAS. UNA VIDA DEL SIGLO XV, by Juan Bautista Avalle-Arce. 1972. (No. 127). -927-8.

AN EDITION OF THE FIRST ITALIAN TRANSLATION OF THE CELESTINA, by Kathleen Kish. 1973. (No. 128). -928-6.

MOLIERE MOCKED: THREE CONTEMPORARY HOSTILE COMEDIES, by Frederick W. Vogler. 1973. (No. 129). -929-4.

INDEX ANALYTIQUE DE "CHATEAUBRIAND ET SON GROUPE LITTERAIRE SOUS L'EMPIRE" DE SAINTE-BEUVE, by Lorin A. Uffenbeck. 1973. (No. 130). -930-8.

THE ORIGINS OF THE BAROQUE CONCEPT OF PEREGRINATIO, by Juergen S. Hahn. 1973. (No. 131). -931-6.

THE "AUTO SACRAMENTAL" AND THE PARABLE IN THE SIXTEENTH AND SEVENTEENTH CENTURIES, by Donald T. Dietz. 1973. (No. 132). -932-4.

FRANCISCO DE OSUNA AND THE SPIRIT OF THE LETTER, by Laura Calvert. 1973. (No. 133). -933-2.

ITINERARIO DI AMORE: DIALETTICA DI AMORE E MORTE NELLA VITA NUOVA, by Margherita de Bonfils Templer. 1973. (No. 134). -934-0.

L'IMAGINATION POETIQUE CHEZ DU BARTAS, ELEMENTS DE SENSIBILITE BAROQUE DANS LA "CREATION DU MONDE," by Bruno Braunrot. 1973. (No. 135). -935-9.

ARTUS DÉSIRÉ, PRIEST AND PAMPHLETEER OF THE SIXTEENTH CENTURY, by Frank Giese 1973. (No. 136). -936-7.

JARDIN DE NOBLES DONZELLAS BY FRAY MARTÍN DE CÓRDOBA, by Harriet Goldberg. 1974. (No. 137). -937-5.

MOLIERE: TRADITIONS IN CRITICISM, by Laurence Romero. 1974 (Essays, No. 1). -001-7.

STUDIES IN TIRSO, I, by Ruth Lee Kennedy. 1974. (Essays, No. 3). -003-3.

LAS MEMORIAS DE GONZALO FERNÁNDEZ DE OVIEDO, Vols. I and II, by Juan Bautista Avalle-Arce. 1974. (Texts, Textual Studies, and Translations, Nos. 1 and 2). -401-2; 402-0.

ESTUDIOS DE LITERATURA HISPANOAMERICANA EN HONOR A JOSÉ J. ARROM, edited by Andrew P. Debicki and Enrique Pupo-Walker. 1975. (Symposia, No. 2). 952-9.

When ordering please cite the *ISBN Prefix* plus the last four digits for each title.

Send orders to:

    University of North Carolina Press
    Chapel Hill
    North Carolina 27514
    U. S. A.

The Department of Romance Studies Digital Arts and Collaboration Lab at the University of North Carolina at Chapel Hill is proud to support the digitization of the North Carolina Studies in the Romance Languages and Literatures series.

www.ingramcontent.com/pod-product-compliance
Lightning Source LLC
Chambersburg PA
CBHW020417230426
43663CB00007BA/1212